A GUIDE TO YOUR ASPIE

ASPERGERS FROM THE INSIDE OUT

FROM THE POPULAR BLOG BY
AMANDA J HARRINGTON

Some material previously available via the Crazy Girl in an Aspie World blog

http://aspie-girl.blogspot.co.uk

ISBN #: 978-1-291-37104-8

CONTENTS

INTRODUCTION

In October, 2012, I was meandering around the house, getting ready to go to work later in the day. It was a drifting sort of day as I was ill and had a temperature. In my haze, as I wondered if I had any socks, I thought how nice it would be to always know where your socks were.

This dreamy thought suddenly propelled into a full internal discussion on how much my Aspergers fiddles with my life in ways large and small. I wondered how other people coped with it and whether they had socks. Then I wondered how many of them knew they were aspies or were living with an aspie and had no idea what to do with them.

In the fugue of my temperature and woozy head, a mad idea was born. I would throw aside my intense need for privacy and start a blog about being an adult woman with Aspergers. I was terrified, readers, petrified at the thought of opening myself up to so many people, all in one go.

The thing is, as soon as the idea was born, I knew I had to do it. Almost as if it had been waiting for me to think it, the idea tumbled into existence and, before I had even tracked down my socks, or prepared for work, or remembered to collect the kids from college, I was sitting at the computer, writing the first two posts.

There was a part of me that sat, dry-mouthed and hyper-ventilating at this point, but I was driven by the idea that I could talk to people and tell them what it was like. If I could describe things well enough, then others might not have to struggle through the years of self-discovery I had endured. And their friends, families and best-beloveds might not have to struggle with them.

And so the Crazy Girl blog became a reality, starting at speed and rarely slowing down since. Readers, if I thought I knew myself before, then I was wrong. You see, by opening myself up to the world, I have also discovered far more about myself. I have revisited my past and been able to look at the other versions of me and feel kindly towards them. I have forgiven myself for getting so many things wrong; I have learned to accept who I am.

I have also realised that there are some things in life that were just meant to be. One of them was that I would be an aspie and another is that I would be able to write about it and help other people understand.

This book is a collection of blog posts covering some of the most fundamental and awkward elements of Aspergers, from both the aspie and non-aspie side of life. The effects of childhood experiences, our dealings with other people, how non-aspies can help us and themselves, all of these and much more are covered. The chapters are based on the blog posts and cluster around general themes, so either settle down with the whole book or dip in and out. And at the very end are some fun posts, including A Guide to your Aspie, which is one of the most popular of all.

My two sons feature quite a lot in my blog and also pop up in this book. IT teen is the non-aspie in the family who has to survive in the random eccentricity caused by two creative, forgetful aspies sharing his space. RT teen is the arty one, who happily drifts through life and often wonders why other people make such a fuss. And then there's me, trying to be a grown up in the middle of it all and still confused when people expect me to be in charge.

I feel very lucky to be able to share this journey with you and your loved ones. I hope it helps you to see things in a new way and to reach out to one another with greater understanding. I also hope it means you can forgive yourself and your beloved if things go wrong. Somewhere, there is always sunshine.

Amanda J Harrington
April 11th, 2013

COMMUNICATION

This is such a big area that I feel like it should have a book of its own. Other people are so immensely important in an Aspergers world but they are also the biggest challenge. You think your aspie is hard to understand? From the other side of the fence, the non-aspie world seems like an absolute morass of hidden agendas, unseen clues, subtle tricks, unusual reactions and harsh words. Viewed like this, is it any wonder that aspies find it difficult to communicate effectively?

I can't emphasise enough the equal difficulties and importance of communication in the aspie world. Imagine the need to have people deal sympathetically with you at the same time as having the ability to alienate yourself and them without even trying. Time and again, aspies see themselves almost from the outside, taking to pieces the very thing that might help them succeed.

The blog posts chosen for this section were hard to narrow down as I've covered communication many times on its own and it also runs, like a silver twisting thread, through everything I've written about Aspergers. I see it as the secret and magical key to dealing with life and all its problems, even though I often find it impossible to solve myself.

Take this section as a guide only, as an example of how things may be done. In every case, each person is an individual who needs their own way of resolving issues. Talk to one another and find your own path through so that you can reach a better understanding and avoid unnecessary drama.

Communication, simply put, is the ability to reach out to other people, even if words are never spoken. Sometimes, all it comes down to is the willingness to make that first move and the hope that everything else will follow.

THE ART OF THE
CONVERSATION-STOPPER

Why people have to make life so complicated, I don't know! I do realise that my aspie viewpoint is uniquely annoying a lot of the time and that I do and say confusing things which make no sense in the normal realm. But in return, when I really get it wrong, day to day, being told *how* and *why* can be a big help, an important step in my ability to understand and try again the next time.

I really do forget things in the middle of conversations. There just doesn't seem to be enough space in the **Current folder** of my brain to keep these things in. As soon as something new comes along, or even the memory of something old, the object I need to keep hold of vanishes over the side of the box and is lost in a dark corner.

In the case of forgetting, it is a genuine forgetfulness. I'm not being careless. I may be distracted, so lose part of a conversation that way, but equally I can interact with you and then still forget what was said in a very short space of time.

Sometimes, this can have a lot to do with how the information is presented. If we were talking about Aunt Aggy's bunions and I was listening, then we skip to another topic, it can be helpful if you come back to Aunt Aggy in a clear way.

Often, when people return, they say something like, 'So, Aunt Aggy was telling me she was going to get them sorted out on Tuesday'. I know this might seem strange but this doesn't help me remember her bunions. To me, it introduces an element of mystery into our conversation. I'm wondering what the unidentified 'them' means in this sentence.

Why? Well, when you first mentioned Aunt Aggy, I registered who she was then moved onto the new topic of the bunions. As they were new, they required more of my attention and were much more interesting than poor Aunt Aggy herself. If you had come back to the subject by saying, 'So, these bunions,' I would have picked up what you meant.

As aspies, we are all about processing and managing information. There is a lot of it and we have to learn all the time, to cope with what people do and say and what happens in life. Conversations in themselves are awkward, even with loved ones, as you never really know where these chats are going. You need to watch them carefully. When they divert, you divert with them, following like a dog following a bouncy red ball. You jet off across the garden and fetch it back.

When the subject changes in a conversation, it's a new blue ball. The other is dropped and forgotten and off we go, after the new ball you want us to chase and bring back. Happily, we pick it up and fetch. There: we've interacted and coped with the conversation. We're standing in front of you with the blue ball, waiting to see what happens with it now.

What happens is, you've already picked up and thrown the red ball in the *other* direction, while we were still running with the blue one. We were facing you when you did it, so you naturally expected us to see it go. But we were concentrating on getting the blue ball back from where it fell, to you.

You stand, looking at us. Why haven't we gone for the red ball? Why are we still all about the blue one? You've finished with the blue one. We look confused and you repeat what you said. Then we realise what you meant, also recognising the irritation as you say it.

Off we go, tail down, willing to fetch the red ball again. Some of the lustre of the game is lost, but we still bring it back. Now, please, if you decide to swap back to that blue one, hold it in the air first and let us see it, before you throw it!

Another conversation-locker is the one where we're talking happily, relaxed and knowing what you and we both mean. This is great; a break from the confusion of what can pass as asperger conversational skills. Suddenly, you look at me and raise an eyebrow. Or your lips thin. Or you blink a few times, pause, then move on.

What was it? What happened? What did I say or do?

I hate this, the inevitable moment when you know you've said or done the wrong thing but have no idea what. This isn't as all-encompassing as the moments when you make a room fall silent. This is like a mini-version of it, but one that stings more deeply a lot of the time, because this often happens with people close to you.

You see, if you're talking to people who don't know you well, they are more likely to stop in their tracks and you have the silent room. But people who do know you are more used to making allowances or re-processing what you just said, to see what you meant to say. Usually, this means they don't make a fuss and just try to carry on as if nothing happened.

The trouble is, we want to *know* what happened! What we said or did. It's a compulsion, really, to find out where we went wrong so we can look at it, roll it over and inspect it, see what it is exactly and how we can deal with it in future. This is the way we deal with the imbalance between what we know and what happens next. Inspection is vital for our peace of mind.

What often happens, though, with our loved ones who have re-acted without explanation, is that they don't want to let us inspect what we did wrong. They want to carry on, so we don't get upset and, sometimes, because they know the whole conversation will be de-railed if we stop to give our attention to the other thing, the one they want to leave behind.

Our loved ones may be feeling hurt themselves - often this is the impression the aspie has of the situation. They don't want to feel any worse by discussing it. And, I'm sorry to say, they do occasionally think we should know what we've said and don't want to repeat it because they think we're trying to get out of trouble by pretending we don't know.

Whatever the reason, I've often fallen foul of saying something within a normal conversation and not being able to find out what it was. I just hate it. It's the equivalent of when you can't hear what a person is telling you and you really want to know, but they won't repeat it. It's rather like the other person is the holder of secrets, or of knowledge. They know what you want to know, but refuse to tell.

This is a conversation-killer, however you look at it. If you were to come out and say, 'Look, I've told you not to bring up my ex-husband!' then we'd know what was wrong and be able to apologise. By not saying and expecting us to know, or by deciding you are not going to share so that we can move on, the niggle of a mystery stirs the muddy waters within and we are now focussing on that, instead of the conversation.

I can guarantee, for the rest of the time we are together, I'll be looking at you, waiting to see if you react again, so I can gather clues as to what I did. I'll be trying to remember exactly what I said, or what I was doing with my body, in case I unconsciously insulted you.

Much, much later, the revelation may descend upon me. A bit like not being able to remember something until you stop trying, the secret of the conversation and your reaction will suddenly reveal itself, when it's too late to resolve it. I'll be left, considering what I did or said and replaying the whole thing, trying to see it from your point of view, so I can work out how hurt or upset you were.

The hurt or upset will be magnified as I fret over it, followed at some stage by anger or irritation that you wouldn't just tell me at the time so I could say sorry or explain what I actually meant.

Don't withhold things from me. Understand that I probably didn't mean what I said, or intentionally forget what we were talking about. This is not a reflection on you, it's simply Me.

I realise this can be an impossible problem, though. How are you supposed to know the difference between when I'm bored or distracted and when I've said something upsetting or shocking for the sake of it? The answer is a very simple one, Reader: **just ask me**.

That's all. If you want to know what I meant or why I did whatever it was, just ask.

And when you divert off into other parts of the conversation, do look back occasionally to make sure I'm following. It can be very strange to see someone zooming along, unhindered by the overgrowth and tree branches. Aspies don't always remember that, to other people, none of these obstacles exist. It's only the aspie who has to fight through to reach the clearing in the centre of the forest. Other people think they're standing in the middle of an open field.

This is why, when you think you've made everything as clear as possible and we're still meandering along, looking confused and wondering where you went, please bear in mind we may not be able to see you through the branches. Call out and give us a helping hand. That way, we'll both reach where we're going a lot faster.

'YOU SAID WHAT?!'

I want to gently butt at the behind of a slightly thorny subject here. I mean to do it gently because I don't want to offend myself too much. This is because I'm going to talk about something which is a particular, shining, glorious and wholly uncontrollable fault of mine. That would be - Saying the Wrong Thing.

Not just saying the wrong thing, mind you. That would be bad enough. How many of us know people who are famed (usually by themselves) for being honest and straight-talking? Yes, honesty is a good thing. Apparently it's also best policy. I'm just not sure how this all manages to unravel and fall apart when that same policy is let loose in the hands of an aspie.

I think what comes unstuck is that an aspie is always honest, except when they're trying to be normal. If an aspie is self-aware enough to know that you cannot, just cannot, tell Mrs Harumph her top lip looks more like Mr Harumph's, then the aspie will seek about for something more obliging to say, while trying not to stare at the bristles on Mrs H's moustache line. Finding nothing that can distract them from the gleaming black hairs standing out in the sunshine, said aspie will then look for stronger measures of distraction and will very likely say something along the lines of, 'Isn't Mr Harumph at home a lot these days?' (he'll have lost his job), or 'Aren't you glad you don't have those kids all over your garden anymore?' (Mrs H will have fallen out with the grandchildren), or, even more likely, 'I keep forgetting to shave!'

This last one is the one that gets me. Not that I tell people I keep forgetting to shave - I'm quite good at remembering, thanks - but when I'm trying to be tactful and avoid talking about something to do with the other person, I'll somehow work it round and bring up that exact subject but make it about *me*. So, you've been grumpy lately? I'll say I'm feeling moody, or that people can't stand to be around me. You look tired, I'll mention feeling old and haggard and various uncomplimentary phrases, which I'll think are okay because I'm talking about me.

Unfortunately, I will be looking and talking to *you*.

Yes, stranger or friend, this is a compulsive habit. I sometimes wonder if it would be better if I just came out and said, 'Blimey, could you be any more difficult to get on with today?!' and leave it at that. Sure, there would be a falling out, possibly an epic one, but it would all be over with at once. Very different from the atmosphere an aspie can build up without even flexing a muscle, when they give in to the tendency to talk around awkward subjects in what they think is a subtle way.

Related to this is my ability to put my foot in it in even more interesting ways. As an example, your teenager neighbour is pregnant and her mother is telling you about it. The keynote speech is full of upbeat optimism, aimed at making the listener aware that the mother of the girl will put up with no criticism or nastiness when it comes to the daughter.

You have no intention of doing either - in general, people with aspergers are pretty open-minded and, having suffered at the hands of others, are willing to live and let live. But this is where the other bane of my conversations comes in. If someone is telling me something and it's obvious I'm not supposed to comment very much on their part of the conversation, I'm so at a loss as to what I can say (chit-chat, a whole other language), that, again, I veer the talk round to me and try to link myself to it in some way.

Please, believe me when I say this isn't meant to build me up or show off. It's simply that other people are a mystery, as is a lot of what goes on around me, but I know more about me so I can talk about me in relation to what you have just said. That way, I contribute to the conversation in a way I am confident will make sense. By referring to myself I am also avoiding the stunned silence reaction, mentioned in an earlier post, where I say what I think is a sensible sentence and afterwards you can hear a pin drop.

So, when trying to be sympathetic and subtle regarding the teen mum, I am likely to talk about my own pregnancies and when my children were babies. So far, so good, but my desire to make this anecdote relevant to the matter in hand will usually divert me off down a tangled path. I'm bound to add comments like, 'but of course I was in my 20s', or 'I had my husband with me' and similar phrases, all of which point to the teen mum being on her own, too young and other matters her mother was trying to avoid when she took the ultra-positive note in the first place.

Do you see what I mean? With the best will in the world, and genuine, kindly intentions, I can still insult the most hardened individuals. Sometimes they won't realise why they feel insulted until afterwards, when they replay the conversation. Then they'll think I'm being snide or looking down at them, or wanting to talk about myself all the time.

It's an absolute minefield. I am still guilty of all the above, especially if I'm tired and not keeping an eye on myself. My coping mechanism these days is to stay quiet if it looks like a tricky conversation. I've learned, partly, to let the other person do the talking so that I am less likely to put my foot in it. This also gives me more time to formulate acceptable, non-offensive answers.

None of this helps all the time, though. It can even make it worse. Picture how attentive I must seem, as I stand, quietly listening, my whole attention on what you are saying (so I know when I'm supposed to talk and can work out what I'm supposed to say). Then , after all that, I slot in a comment I think is fine and it's one of my humdingers. That is worse because you have built up confidence in me as a listener and as a person, only to find I've waited all that time to verbally slap you up the side of the head. And then, to make it worse, I stand and smile, patiently waiting for you to carry on - as if I had never insulted you at all! How brazen I am, how hard-faced!

Oh dear, I do try. I want to be nice to people and I want to have conversations. I just don't want your mouth to drop open and for us both to end up blushing as I realise I've excelled myself, yet again, alienating someone who thought they would like to talk to me.

I should add that true friends, who know me well enough, they still take offence but they also give me the benefit of the doubt. They recognise the innocent expression that accompanies the insult. They often replay what I said, to themselves if not to me, and see how there is more than one way to take it. Then we have another cup of tea and a piece of cake and carry on talking.

You see, it's amongst these snippets of me trying to listen and be normal and include myself in conversations, that the real gold can be found. If you can get past that first red herring, flapping about on the coffee table next to the gingerbread, then you can carry on and have a really good, brilliant, gold-leaf covered conversation that will stay with you until you see each other again.

In other words, keep the faith and keep talking: it's worth it for the wisdom of the aspie, buried beneath the odd words, the tumbling logic and the strange fascination they have with your top lip.

SHOW, DON'T TELL?

The rule in fiction, apparently, is show don't tell. The idea is that rather than explain what your character feels and thinks, you write a storyline which shows the reader these things.

I never quite understood this, as some of the best books I've read have a narration element, where the writer steps outside of the story and speaks directly to the reader. What about Jane Eyre, that staple of ailing TV companies?

Reader, I married him.

Jane, or rather Charlotte Bronte, speaks in the first person, so is allowed to take the extra step and admit that her reader exists with this line. Terry Pratchett does it all the time, as part of his story, in the added footnotes in many of his stories. No one seems to have taken them outside and given them a talking to.

Life is like this, too, I think, which is why most people want fiction to follow. People like to be *shown* things and like to *do* things. They don't want the talking to get in the way. Often, the explanations are unnecessary as, in life, you exist and move and do and are probably about to live out the event you'd be talking about.

This is where aspies fall foul, you see. This is the point I'm leading up to (I'm giving you clear narration there, reader, and I'm speaking directly to you).

Aspies would quite like a narration in life. For one thing, it would stop them getting more than half of the blooming thing wrong, and would certainly avoid a lot of those stunned silences and people blinking in surprise. It would also avoid going into massively hasty decisions without your eyes open.

You may still decide you need that high-end computer, with extras, plus the excitement bundle at a one-day-only offer; but if you had a gentle narrator in the background who could explain that the computer is great, but tomorrow you have the rent to pay, then life might be less complicated.

I agree that aspies are pretty bad at listening to advice at times, and other times we listen too much. For an impulse decision, like the computer, we can be extremely, atrociously bad at listening to sensible advice. We wants it now!!

When it comes to what you should do in your emotional or social life, I don't know about the rest of you, but I tend to gather all the advice I can because I have no idea what I'm doing. The end result can be that I do something entirely different from what I should have done and end up more confused than ever.

And anyway, I have to hold my hand up here as being one of those aspies who does already have the inner narration. I know this is true of so many others too. Unfortunately, it is not the narration of an omnipresent narrator who can advise us sagely because they know the whole story. No, it's our own voices, the narration built up from a lifetime of wondering what to do next.

With me, it would be less of the 'Reader, I married him,' than 'Reader, I spent all his money on this fabulous business idea that was bound to succeed, then I lost interest and me and his daughter spent the rest of *my* money on a weekend at the theme park because I'd forgotten her birthday, so it was only fair, and then I left him because he became really bad tempered and snappy all the time and was making my life miserable.'

It's true of all of us that if we had a kindly author in the background, manufacturing our lives so that we reached a happy conclusion. there would be less bankruptcy and more quiet marriages with country gentlemen. There would also, probably, be more tragic deaths of surplus cousins, siblings and ailing mothers, or is it that I just read too much 19th century literature?

I still hold to it, though: aspies need the narration. It's no good expecting us to work out, from using our senses, what is going on and what we're supposed to do next. We don't see that straight line between cause and effect, we're too distracted by the noise going on between them to work it out. We need the cause and effect explained, or at least for someone to ask if we get it.

Actually, no, don't ask if we get it either, because we'll say we do. Part of the problem is that we think we do understand and act accordingly, still not linking up cause and effect and only going with what feels right or seems logical at the time. This is part of the reason we find it so difficult to explain afterwards, so many decisions are based on gut instinct at any given time, and are then lost on the wind and forgotten.

If possible, aspies, do remember to ask for a bit of narration. A few words can go a long way. And non-aspies and best beloveds, do remember to offer those few words. Yes, I know you sometimes (or often) get them thrown back at you impatiently - we *know* what we're doing! - but persevere because it will probably mean less high-end computing and more money for the rent.

As for the showing and not telling, every day, in confused looks, hesitant words, mumbled explanations and quick glances across the room, we aspies show and don't tell you how we're feeling and what we're doing. It's up to you, as the reader, to work it out without needing us to narrate it for you.

CONVERSATIONS WITH AN ASPIE

I recently had a conversation with RT teen about his plans to leave college. I wanted the conversation to be a simple, clear one where we could talk about him staying on and trying the next level of his Art course. Instead, it went something like this:

Me: So, about you leaving college.

RT teen: When?

Me: In summer, when your course finishes.

RT teen: It starts again in September, for level 3.

Me: But you said you were leaving in Summer, that you didn't want to do level 3.

RT teen (indignant): I did not!

Me: You even told your tutor that the course wasn't what you expected and you weren't doing level 3.

RT teen (pausing): Oh yes.

Me: So, you changed your mind?

RT teen: About what?

Me (teeth gritted): About level 3! You want to do it now??

RT teen: No! I don't want to do level 3.

Me: But you said you did?!

RT teen: When?

Me: Just now! When we were talking about it!

RT teen: I don't remember saying that, you know I don't like the course.

(I will insert a small pause here while I resisted the urge to cuff him round the ears, like a mother cat and wherein I relayed the above conversation back to him, with italics inserted in a great many places).

RT teen: Oh. Well, I think I changed my mind. I'll give level 3 a go.

Me: You'd better tell your tutor then.

RT teen: Why?

Me: Because she thinks you're finishing.

RT teen: No, she doesn't. I never said I was.

Readers, I will stop at that point, there is no need for you to suffer any further. Anyway, some minutes later we had ascertained that RT teen was definitely maybe considering staying on for level 3 and understood the need to tell his poor tutor, who was, for reasons best known to herself, labouring under the false assumption that he didn't want to do level 3 and would be leaving in summer.

This conversation was like a merry-go-round, a real-life version of the communications roundabout that is aspergers meeting aspergers meeting life. I usually follow RT teen's logic and reasoning and structure what I say to match, but this day nothing I said seemed to help at all. I held onto my patience by the skin of my teeth, remembering all the times I must have driven other people mad in a similar way.

We did get to the bottom of it but it struck me as a very good example of how communication can falter even within just a few sentences. RT teen was tired, so there was more reason than normal for confusion to creep in, but this odd way of thinking and mis-remembering is probably often going on inside the aspie, even when the outside seems more sensible.

You may have a much easier conversation with your aspie than I did, then come back later and discover they remembered everything differently to the way it actually happened. This is where arguments start as your memory of the event and the aspie's memory differ widely enough for it to be like you were talking to some other person who just looked like them.

In mine and RT teen's case, we were further mishandled by both being aspie and my needing to get to the bottom of the matter, so that we could move forward on his college plans. I guess, sometimes, we are all guilty of giving up in the middle of an aspified conversation and telling ourselves we'll come back to it later. When we really need to have the conversation and reach some kind of conclusion, then we must struggle on and make the best of things.

RT teen *did* want to leave the conversation until he was less tired but I didn't dare. What if I forgot to talk to him about it for another week and then he missed a deadline for applying? What if I forgot for longer and ended up having to call college and talk to his tutor, trying to sort it all out after the event?

All these things have happened before and I couldn't trust myself or him to remember at the right time and deal with it, without some mishap befalling us. So, the above is what can happen if you have to force a conversation at a time when the aspie is at once with you and away from you, one half of them walking alongside you, dogs running off ahead and leads swinging from your hands, the other half of them stuck firmly in some other place, which moves secretly beside this one and steals away their attention.

By plugging away, going over the same ground and impressing upon RT teen that yes, we did need to talk about it now, *right now*, we made it through to the end of the conversation with a decision in place. And on Monday morning, when I brought it up again, the decision had held fast and he spoke to his tutor.

Sometimes, you just can't force the issue and talk things through. If the mood is not right, the attention isn't there or more than half of the aspie is stuck in the other place, then that conversation is not going to work in the right way. What you might have to do is come back to it later (and remember to do so), hoping that your aspie has some recall of the failed conversation so that you don't have to start from scratch.

As an aspie who is very good at forgetting and does 'lose' whole conversations, I know how frustrating it can be from the other side of things, to know other people need to communicate with you - and *have* communicated with you - but then your mind has lost the lot of it and you either pretend to know what they're talking about or admit, yet again, you have no idea.

I've done both - pretending and admitting. Pretending is a high-risk strategy that causes all kinds of problems whereas admitting so often ends up in a telling off. It makes the other person feel you had no interest in them or the conversation and that you only pretended to listen.

Yes, erm, sometimes I actually *do* pretend to listen, or drift off and give the appearance of listening as an automatic response. But mostly I try to take it all in, even if it leaves, quickly, by a side entrance, as soon as the show has ended.

The only thing you can do with your aspie, if it's important, is mention it more than once. You know by this I mean mention it many times. You do risk the aspie moaning and eye-rolling, saying they *know* all that and so on. Put up with it because they're still likely to forget.

Spoken communication is a two-way device, put forward as a way to save on head-butting and stick-waving in primeval times. Sometimes, you may be tempted to revert to those times and see if poking the aspie with a stick as you talk will help them remember what you're telling them but, trust me, they will only remember how horrid you are and burn the stick later.

(I know this as a very old lady friend of mine had a son in his 60s who she felt needed some 'reminding' with her walking stick as she told him things. It would snake through the chairs and poke him on the leg but he became expert at jigging his legs about so she couldn't always catch him and he still managed to have the conversation his way. Sticks do not work, even if you are a highly intelligent 90 year old).

Dogged determination and patience will win the day. Be brave about setting off the aspie moan, tell them things more than once, only remind them what they have said if it is necessary. Be constant and consistent in your attentions, to give your aspie the best chance of remembering what you are talking about and also anything important you decide.

In the end, also be humorous, dear readers. You need all the humour you can get when you have to face troublesome aspie conversations. Take it in the spirit of a creative episode in the middle of dull, everyday life and be glad that not everyone you know can remember what they said last Tuesday. Or any Tuesday.

MIS-LISTENINGS AND THE
RAVINE OF NO SENSE

I wanted to touch upon what it can be like to speak the language of aspie. This is a switch that clicks on and off, mostly accidentally, like when you lean on the cooker and are only saved from total conflagration by the built-in safety settings.

The switch is not the same mechanism which causes a total shutdown - this is the switch that controls communication. It has what I like to think of as, the Babel effect. At any given moment, on a whim, it clicks on or off and the aspie can no longer understand their language of choice. They are now separated from other people by a great divide, a chasm to be crossed only when the time is right.

For aspies, the switch can be triggered by their own feelings on any given day, or more likely, by other people leaning on it. Unlike the cooker, aspies tend to have very limited built-in safety settings, which usually comprise of removing themselves from the situation, throwing objects and shouting before removing themselves or turning away and having a total shutdown.

This idea that an aspie brain can suddenly change the settings and not receive information in a normal way, is one I only know about from personal experience. Forgive me if this one doesn't resonate so strongly with other aspies (though I have a feeling it will). Let me give you the example which best describes it from my point of view.

One of my many failed jobs was in a doctor's office, on the reception desk. As usual, for reasons I can never really explain, I had decided to go for a job which involved lots and lots of contact with other people. Now I would maybe know better. Maybe not, too, I seem to enjoy the pursuit of unsuitable goals.

This reception job had its ups and downs and the incident I want to describe was very early in the experience. I was feeling pretty stressed overall, as it involved early starts, it needed attention to detail under pressure, there was an intercom which, frankly, scared me and the phones would ring at the same time as lots of people talking. All very confusing and overwhelming - what was I thinking?!

On this particular day, an older gent came in, a friend of one of the doctors. He was making a social call and wanted me to let his friend know he was here. I don't remember how stressed I was at that moment, it must have been bad. I do remember realising who he was (I'd been told to expect him) and leaning forward as he came to the desk and started speaking.

He spoke, readers. He spoke English, in a loud enough voice to hear over everything else. I saw his lips move and heard his voice. I listened attentively. **I understood nothing he said.** He might as well have been standing there saying, 'Blurble urble urble oooo,' over and over again.

For a moment, after he finished speaking, I stood, perplexed. Then horrified, as I realised I hadn't understood even one word. Amongst this was a stirring of fear too, as he was looking expectantly at me, waiting for me to act on what he had said. Desperately, my face blushing a deep red, I bent towards him and asked him to repeat himself.

He was angry and irritated, which I do understand. He was also keen to share the feelings and started by asking me if I was stupid or deaf or both? Then he repeated what he had just said, loudly, angrily and slowly, glaring at me the whole time and slapping his hand on the counter.

I understood the second time and told the doctor his friend had arrived. It was awful, though. A part of me knew I couldn't have done anything differently, I couldn't make my ears work the way they were meant to - or, more accurately, my brain work the way it should. I was stuck with the situation and I just had to hope it didn't happen again.

There was also a part of me that knew the man didn't have to be so unpleasant about it. I was human, I had been mistaken in not understanding him but I didn't do it to upset him or inconvenience him. Often, though, in public-facing roles, common courtesy and decency are left at the door, only to be used for proper people, ones who don't wear name tags and who get paid more per hour than the lowly shop-worker, receptionist, cleaner and so on (I've done all those jobs and the main benefit is you get to see the best of people as well as the worst).

Without breaching any confidentiality, I must say that I also met a man who had lots of problems, some self-inflicted and some not. He would come into the surgery, obviously struggling against his problems and having difficulty restraining his aggressive and out-of-control emotions. He would arrive at the desk and physically contain himself, looking away, concentrating on other things, on any thing at all, so that he could control the way he spoke to me. That man did everything in his power to appear respectful and to treat me well for the short (but to him very long) time he needed to speak to me.

I respected him, for his efforts and for his recognition that we all deserve to be treated decently. I also recognised the way he behaved as an obvious, very much outward version of how I coped with things myself when trying to communicate under difficult circumstances. He was mirroring what I also do, using my strength and concentration, such as it is, to focus on things other than the person I am talking to, so that I can continue talking to that person without running out of the room or screaming as I bang my head against a wall. Sometimes you need to focus on the irrelevant details to carry on dealing with the main event.

Back to the different language problem. I believe that, like so many other problems in aspergers, it is set off by stressful situations. You just have to divert your energies, your brain activity, your self in general, away from the frightening thing which is trying to happen right in front of you. Your aspie brain thinks if it can divert you for long enough, you will be safe. So, even when you don't want to be diverted, you are and you find yourself in one of those vicious circles of needing to understand something, not being able to understand it, becoming too stressed to understand it, and then round again.

I'm not saying all aspies change the language received from the language spoken. That was a very specific instance that happened to me and is set apart in my mind. But I know similar things happen a lot, where you do understand the words spoken, you just can't grasp their meaning.

On occasion, when I've asked people to repeat things to me a few times, I've resorted to asking them to spell it out. Then there is a moment while I relay the letters back, building up the required word in my mind. Then it makes sense, it becomes what it was meant to be.

Also, when I talk about stressful situations, don't be confused here. I know you will have had times when similar things have happened with your aspie, and you've been in the comfort of your own home, without stresses like I had at the doctor's surgery. So, where is the stress there, you wonder. What causes the mis-listening then?

Oh, reader, what causes it is Stuff. Big stuff, little stuff, stuff from last week we never processed to our satisfaction, the feeling we had yesterday evening that reminded us of the bad thing that happened ten years ago.

Or maybe a few little bits of stuff have followed us around all week and we've been fine, we have, we've done everything that was expected of us and then all the bits of stuff caught up at the same time and tumbled together to bump against the backs of our legs at just the wrong moment. And it's the moment you say the important thing, or the thing that becomes important because we have no idea what you're talking about.

It's frustrating that the stresses which make our switches flick on and off can be so blooming well small and stupid, so tiny we didn't even notice them and could never tell you what they were. It's like grit blowing in the air in front of your face; if there is enough of it, some of it is bound to get in your eyes; but you couldn't say which particles blew in, only that there was a whole cloud of it that you didn't see until you were blinking back the tears.

As usual, the key to all this is patience. Be patient, explain yourself, use different words if necessary. Only raise your voice to repeat the words if we ask you to. Don't throw the TV remote at us when we ask why you're shouting. If necessary, spell it out. Describe the word as if you've forgotten the name, that's often how we explain things to you.

On top of all that, be gentle and smile away the mis-listening. It can be frightening, to not understand. When so many other things are confusing and misleading, not knowing what you say, our beloved, that can be terrifying. There's a small part of us that always worries we'll lose you too, like we lose the little things in life.

Be like me when I watched the distressed man using the pins of the noticeboard to distract his aching mind: admire the effort that goes into communicating and try to ignore the frustration evident in our eyes. Frustration belongs with the small stuff. In the end it's just emotional grit and a few tears and a kind touch can soon fix it all up.

THE SOCIABLE ASPIE?

Aspergers and social go together like a pony and trap. Unfortunately, the pony is usually running away down the hill with the trap bouncing along behind, doing a mad dance and deciding if it's about to break into pieces.

In my experience, many aspies are social creatures, willing to go out into the world to meet others and make friends. The ability to actually do that is what seems to fail; or rather, the ability to do it and successfully maintain it.

In my own world, I can talk to people and make friends, or at least be friendly, like anyone else. The reality is that I am shrinking away on the inside, waiting for the encounter to be over so I can scurry off and not be stressed any more. On the outside, I appear friendly and approachable, whereas the inside is a quivering wreck.

Other aspies genuinely want to be sociable and can mix in groups and have no problem talking to people. The difficulties arise in what they say and how they say it or how they behave. The aspie is a unique, individualistic force in a social situation. Rather like seeing smoke rising from the trees, you may often be able to tell where the aspie is in a crowded room, even if you can't see them.

The need and desire to be sociable is often at odds with what the aspie can achieve, in terms of being social with people who have no understanding of Aspergers. I don't want to be glum about it - lots of aspies have friends and enjoy social situations. But even these social types come up against familiar problems, which I have outlined in the following chapters.

I would always say, if your aspie is sociable, then support them going out and meeting people, even if they have a tendency to create problems. For all the times when people react badly or make us feel small, there will be those we meet who become lifelong, steadfast, wonderful friends.

For the aspie who would rather hole up in their room and never set a foot outside the door? Have hope, for there may be online friends who mean as much to them as anyone you know in the real world. And I have to tell you, sad as it seems to you to see your aspie closeted away, for those of us who prefer it this way, that peace and serenity is like gold in the middle of a tattered world.

SOCIAL OR ANTI-SOCIAL?

This is a bit like asking, milk and sugar? You can't just say, yes, please; you need to be more specific.

Aspergers is the social form of autism - I feel like smacking whoever says that. I've often said it myself, in fact, when trying to explain to people:

1. Why my son can have aspergers and still want to be friends with their child

2. How being sociable *can* be expressed by climbing the wall and falling on the group of children you want to be friends with.

(I exaggerate slightly there, he missed them by inches).

Sociability, in the normal world, can be something like a James Bond movie, all glitz, glamour, attractive people and plenty of allure. Or it can be the sweet little girl-child who brings you a daisy-chain and says she made it for you. It can be the little old ladies at the checkout, making best friends with the shop assistant, or the college kids, making best friends for life with everyone they meet in their first week.

Sociability has many faces, even in a normal world, but there are still acceptable rules. It's these rules which can confuse the aspie, child or adult, often because they aren't obvious, or written down anywhere.

I remember poring over the pages of my girl's magazines, looking for the secret of success, in life, relationships, boys, fashion, you name it. I didn't really find it. What I did find was a lot of confusing information.

Like with boys, (cringing here, sorry various girl's magazines, but really?), you always have to look your best when you go out, but you also have to be yourself and be natural. Boys know when you're being fake. As well as that, you don't want to wear too much make up, but here's the make up you need if you want to look like you're not wearing any (what??).

For relationships, the advice is much the same: you need to talk and be completely honest with each other, but you also need to have some mystery (as I'm a mystery even to myself I never had any trouble with this one). You need to work as a team, but keep separate interests (some of the happiest couples I know do everything together).

And so on. Advice, advice, advice. This is what confused me most. Those unwritten rules of social interaction, they *were* written, weren't they, in girl's and women's magazines? I took that to mean they were true. After all, they were written by people in the know and the pages smelled nice, so it must be true.

I sometimes reflect on the advice about looking your best as I'm dragging my sorry self round Tesco, trying to remember if the part of my leg that's visible looks like it belongs to a wolf-woman. I'll eventually peek to see if it does and then, sometimes, I shrug and just buy my milk. Life somehow gets in the way of effortless make up and glamorous clothes.

I also shrink from all the social advice on how to deal with other people. For years I soaked it up, trying to work out what I could do to make it all better. I wanted to learn, so that I could manage others, and maybe enjoy them too. I did enjoy my friends, that was a blast and was easy. I just couldn't understand why I was okay with them but not with humanity at large.

I finally realised the secret of this a few months ago. It's because **your friends care about you, so you feel safe**. After growing up in the modern world and trying to forge a life in an alien environment, it soon becomes clear that a lot of the people you meet do not care about you, so you don't feel safe. It is simple really.

By feeling safe, you are yourself and can enjoy the company of others. It's a liberating concept and one that has put to rest many years of feeling those magazines had got the better of me and left me in a barren landscape of no social skills and hairy legs.

I can now say, with certainty, that I don't really give a fig for the unwritten rules of social conduct. Those rules can go climb their own wall. I'm sticking with the people who are still pleased to see me when I'm not looking my best and who don't mind if I forget to ask them if they want milk and sugar. They're the ones who prove that aspergers *is* the sociable form of autism, simply because with friends, anyone can be sociable because they feel safe.

TOO MUCH PEOPLE!

No, before you get out the red pen, I haven't lost my grammatical manners - well, not all of them anyway. Today, I want to bring up the tricky subject of Too Much People. I don't mean there are too many people (that's a debate for a different kind of blog); rather, there is too much to be had of People in general. Let me explain.

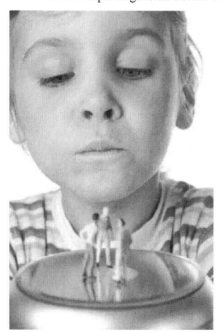

People in the personal sense are bad enough, especially on prickly days. Your loved ones can drive you to distraction. They can be too focused on stuff you need to do, like remembering to thank old Mrs Edwards for her card and not run and hide behind the hedge when she opens the door. They can even get on your last nerve when they want nothing from you except a civil good morning. If this is how you are feeling, can you imagine what it's like to then have to face people you *don't* love? Or like? Or even know??

I've gathered, from my vague meandering into the minds of non-aspies, that people in the street, the shops, at the school gate and in other cars on the roads, are not usually considered a type of social contact. As far as I can work out, to non-aspies, social contact is when you actually talk to people, or touch them. It can also be things like chatting to strangers in the queue or on the next table in the cafe.

What non-aspies don't count is the general hubbub of society as it mills around you in its many forms. They can walk along a street with their best-beloved and not be distracted by the myriad faces around them or the sound of other voices. I think this is a kind of non-aspie focusing arrangement.

As an aspie, it's also possible to walk down a busy street and notice none of these things, but this is often only if you are already alone and have zoned out. Or you aren't alone but have zoned out anyway.

In a more normal frame of mind, where you're plugged in enough to talk to people and let them talk back, walking down the street is similar to being surrounded by pockets of sound, let loose by tiny orchestras, or by sudden thunder, followed by hail. It's very difficult to ignore other people if you are already paying attention to someone. You're completely switched on.

If I'm trying to concentrate on what someone is saying to me in the middle of the cafe, but behind them there is an elderly couple talking about what the neighbour saw on Friday night, then that's it. I have to know what she did see on Friday night. That's kind of fun.

If the same scenario has a crowd of women talking on the next table, not being loud or disruptive, just chatting, then that's not so fun. A bigger, more confusing noise can be like trying to talk in a noisy club. I can look at the person I'm with and listen to them, and I can catch the drift of the conversation, but imagine doing that with the noise of the club all around you. Distracting isn't it?

It's not just distracting though. Some days, days when I should perhaps have looked outside, then closed the door and stayed where I was - on those days, it's not good to see all the other people around me. It won't matter where I go or what I do, unless I live on my desert island or Scottish hillside, there will be other people in the day.

Each one can be a sharp blast of sound on the senses, cold rain down the back of your shirt. Like being slapped, hard, with a cold hand. Even the sight of other people on a bad day can have me shivering and wanting to be alone.

They don't have to *do* anything, you understand. I can be alone amongst them, no need to talk, no reason for them to even look at me. But they are there and I look at *them*. I listen to them. I avoid them as their presence seems greater than it should be, my personal space being invaded as they pass by. They have become bigger, they feel as if they come closer, I must take notice of them.

I think it's partly the need to spot danger that sets this off. If I'm having a bad day, then I already feel vulnerable, so going out into the world seems much more risky than before. As people are on my list of known dangers anyway, seeing them on a vulnerable day is like laying myself open to harm.

If I must go out when I feel like this, I try to avoid any sort of contact. Again, I would point out that my version of contact and a non-aspie one will be very different. It's days like this that I love those self-service tills in shops, self-service petrol stations, anything where I can minimise contact.

From the outside, I feel it must be obvious that I'm different, though perhaps I just look more eccentric? I'm sure my footsteps must be quicker, the actual steps closer together as I dash across the shop. I hope my stony-faced expression conceals the panic under the surface. I try not to look around because I know once I start looking, I won't be able to stop.

Back in the car, and, for a moment, panic subsides as I clutch the wheel and drop my bag behind the seat. The shop is over, now recover and do what comes next. It doesn't matter what comes next, be it more social contact or simply going home: I still need to recover before I leave.

I'll tell you the image that comes to mind most often when I'm feeling this way: a cheese grater. Sorry if you're squeamish, or have a good imagination, but the feeling I get from other people can be like having the world rub me up against the grater. It's sharp, painful, damaging. On a better day, when things haven't got to bad, it might be more like sandpaper.

You can see why, if I feel like this, that I sometimes have a Too Much People day. The trouble is, if you give in to your instincts and stay at home, or in your safe place, then one TMP day can lead to another and another. It becomes easier to avoid them more than you see them.

It's not hard to see how you can move from there to a place where you spend more time apart from the world than in it. As an aspie, this feels more natural, as you're always set apart in some way. An increase in separateness can be a blessed relief, a chance to relax, knowing you don't have to try to be normal enough to fit in.

Another small step from there and you would barely go out at all and it would soon become harder to deal with the people you do see, even though you know and trust them. Logic rules here and if you wean yourself away from people, then you do end up living without them.

It's a hard choice, though. Believe me when I say, I understand the temptation to live the life of the hermit, in a modern sense, with internet shopping and yourself for company. I see it as it can be: tranquillity, a blending of you and your environment in a way that doesn't happen when you're constantly striving to live by society's rules.

Be careful, dear aspie. It is tranquil, so peaceful. There are no distractions, no sudden noises, no sharp rain down the back of the shirt. How comfortable it is, how easy.

Except, so is falling asleep in the snow and look where that gets you. It's quite possible to be so cold you start to feel warm and, before you know it, what you used to recognise as danger becomes a welcoming relief.

Don't close the door every day. Watch out for the TMP days and do what you can to alleviate the stress. As always, be kind to yourself. But not so kind that you shut the door altogether.

Those pesky people in their awkward world, full of noise, awash with drama, always seeming to want something from you and never giving you the right keys to their own mysteries: you need them and they need you. This is one of the mysteries of life.

For all the noise and drama and cold rain, we all need each other and to be without that social contact, even if it is just the chatting in the queue, is to lose a part of yourself that can be very hard to reclaim.

Close the door, dear aspie. Lock it if you must. Then on the next day, open it again and see how things look. Don't assume the weather hasn't changed from the day before. If you can, go out and come back in again. Exercise your People muscle, don't let it wither.

You see, some days will be People Days, without the TM part. It doesn't matter how thorny you are, or how unlikely it seems. Keep opening the door and going out and you will have People Days. Just don't forget your umbrella, as there is always going to be cold rain sometimes. And don't fall asleep in the snow.

THE SOCIALLY AWKWARD
ASPIE

Okay, why not just say that most aspies are shy? And that the ones who aren't are the exception. Would it be truer than saying aspies are socially awkward?

I'm not convinced. I am shy, I always have been, but plenty of people are shy without being on the spectrum. My son, when he was young, was the opposite of shy. Sometimes, I would have preferred him to be a bit shy and less likely to burst into groups of people, ready to make friends, no matter what.

Is it truer then, to say aspies are socially awkward rather than simply shy? NO, it isn't. Let me be firm about this: being socially awkward is totally different from being shy or from being too extroverted. I can prove it.

Let's see. If you're shy, you don't feel comfortable making new friends as you worry how they will behave and you don't know what to say. But once you've made friends, you're not shy anymore because you feel comfortable now and don't need to worry as much.

If you're socially awkward, you can still make friends but that won't stop you behaving inappropriately or oddly the next time you see them. You may be friends, but you'll still ask them why they had such a bad hair cut or you'll get distracted and peel the stickers off their brand new bag.

As aspies, we often hit the jackpot in social relationships because we're usually socially awkward to begin with, then shy on top of that. Imagine it, readers, not only do we have the talent to offend without trying, we can also do it at the same time as dying a thousand deaths because we have to speak in public! How extraordinarily interesting we are!

As for the extroverted aspie, it seems that being socially awkward is even more exciting for them than the shy aspie. At least the shy aspie has some chance of not showing themselves up as mostly they daren't speak or interact anyway, so they don't have the opportunity. The extrovert, though, has ample opportunity and makes great use of it.

As I've said, when my son was small, he loved to make friends. If he was going somewhere for the first time, he had a habit of entering the room, his top half hunkered down, arms swinging and gorilla noises coming out of him. It was an easy way for everyone in the room to see him at the same time. He would then straighten up, laugh and run into the group, usually tickling people on their faces as he passed.

I have to admit, this unconventional method made him plenty of friends. Little boys love this kind of thing and it was a shortcut to helping him find out quickly which children would be friends with him. Also, it made it easier for me, his ultra-shy mother, to enter the room with him as all eyes were on him instead of me.

As an adult extrovert, most aspies don't subscribe to the animal impressions or face tickling. Perhaps this is a mistake as it would probably still work as a way to quickly sort friend from foe. Extroverts have their outgoing personalities on show and, logically, they also show their awkwardness too. If someone doesn't mind who they speak to and isn't always worrying about what they say, then it soon becomes apparent if they start to do or say things outside the norm.

There is a man who works as a salesman in a shop near here. He's extremely sociable and it would never occur to him not to speak or make conversation with customers. They probably have to lock him in the back room when it comes time for his break. He's a very good salesman, if you don't mind the wall of friendliness that descends on you when he approaches.

I'm not too happy with personal-space invaders, but I must admit I knew of him at school and his personality has always burst into a room ahead of him. I was in the shop one day when he wanted to help a very cultured looking middle-aged lady. He bellowed across the shop at her, to ask if he could help. She flinched and told him she wanted to make a payment for something.

He rushed to the other end of the counter, where the card machine was and patted it hard, saying to her, 'Come on! Come over here then!', for all the world like she was the family dog at tea-time. She blinked at him, her eyes bright with shock and her face rigid. Then, because he has the sort of personality you don't ignore, she went and she paid.

It would never have occurred to him that she might be offended by his approach. He had no intention of upsetting her and only wanted to help, but on the surface he appeared loud and brash. She probably came away wondering why she hadn't spoken up to him.

I use this man as an example of how an extroverted personality can still be socially awkward - as well as unaware of the fact. It's a happier state than the perennially fretful shy aspie, who always wants to do things right but is hampered from doing anything at all.

The trouble with aspies, shy or extrovert, is that they have the full potential to do the wrong thing, in word or deed, but only some ability to recognise when they have done it. It's no wonder that worry becomes so familiar! Imagine not knowing when you've done or said the wrong thing, even when someone has pointed it out to you? It's like learning new rules, except the rules are always changing so you can never keep up.

And that's what it's like: constantly changing rules. To a non-aspie, the rules of social behaviour are learned and then become obvious, so that if they do end up making a mistake, they know what it was. To an aspie, each occasion is different and can only be viewed from what we have learned so far. We can hope that the situation is similar enough to a past one so that we know what to do and say, but then if things change or we get confused, the past situation no longer seems relevant and we're on our own again.

Rules learned once are stored, as much as possible. It's just tricky fitting the rules in our heads to the life being lived in front of us. It's like playing snap with a lightning-quick ten year old - you know you're never, ever going to win but you have to play.

It's impossible to match up the rules with the situation quickly enough to make them work. Half the time, it's guess-work. If the situation is simple or very familiar, then it should be fine. If it's an unfamiliar situation or it seems stressful, then we can't always remember the right rules, at least not in time for them to be useful.

This goes some way to explaining why quite a few aspies are very well-mannered. It's been said that aspies can seem old-fashioned in their manners. That's because manners can be learned, the rules are pretty simple. When someone does something for you, you thank them. When they thank you for something, you say 'you're welcome'. When you want something, you say please.

If you appreciate how aspies can learn these rules, then you see why we stick to them so closely. We know we can do these ones, we have these down. It falls apart slightly if we have to thank you for something we didn't want, as a thwarted alligator would be more genuine, but we still say it.

I use the same approach to help me through social situations that are more demanding. Always have manners, you see, as they help enormously. So, at the checkout or when meeting new people (yikes!), I can make small talk because it's polite to do that. I sometimes struggle for a subject, as my brain likes to slot in inappropriate conversation-starters, but if I can keep an eye on that tendency, then it's pretty easy to chat.

I've seen people look surprised when I talk to them. I think it's because, before I opened my mouth, I probably looked quite severe and serious - intimidating, even. They didn't know that the reason for my expression was the concentration it took for me to have a run at speaking to them and also, the thought involved in everyday living.

What I do like is that people respond when you chat. These days, it's not that common for strangers to have little conversations and people usually enjoy it if it happens. I also come away with a new sense of accomplishment because I've spoken to someone I didn't know and made them smile. It helps the day go well and it also helps to remember these times when the day goes down the drain, along with the house key.

There's no solution to being socially awkward, except for learning rules that help, rather than trying to learn rules for every situation. We have to accept that we're never going to fit perfectly into general society - there's always going to be a slight squeezing sound as we struggle to slip through the gaps in the fence while everybody else uses the gate.

Now, years after realising I didn't quite fit, I take heart from the fact that there are many other people who don't fit either, and some of them are my brightest and best friends. It doesn't matter if we get it wrong, we just have to move on and try not to dwell on the temporary mortification of the moment.

We can be different and also social, even the shyest of us. All it takes is practice and a belief that there will always be people who are willing to open themselves up to us and be our friends, even if we never meet them again.

To corner-hiders and face-ticklers everywhere, *thank you* for reading my blog and *please* visit again!

INAPPROPRIATE HONESTY

'Inappropriate behaviour' - the number of times I heard this when my son was growing up, mainly from his teachers. Now, don't get me wrong, he wasn't doing anything really bad here, at least not the kind of things which always sprung into my mind when they used the word inappropriate. And, compared to me trying to burn down the school, I always thought RT teen's childhood exploits were pretty tame.

I guess the thing is, as a little boy, he kept on with the inappropriate behaviours. He was very inventive and each day would bring some new thing he had done. Some of them were dangerous, some were funny, most were simply annoying - no one can be annoying like an aspie can. Nearly every day, after school, I would stand and listen to his catalogue of disasters, with the teacher talking about him while he stood there, head bowed as he listened.

I had two main gripes with this: that she always talked about my son while he was present and that she always told me what he had done when it was too late for me to act on it. Perhaps if they'd called me in when he was plastering the little girl head to toe with mud then I could have impressed upon him that it hadn't been a great idea?

The problem is that most schools expect children to behave themselves a certain way and to be semi-independent of their parents. By semi-independent, I mean they don't want the child to bawl or throw up when separated from mum and dad and they do expect the child to hold their water until they reach the toilet. The other thing schools mainly want is as little parental involvement as possible, while maintaining an illusion of the parents being involved in their child's schooling.

This was never more apparent to me than when mini-RT teen got up to his high jinks. Yes, I sympathised with the teacher that it wasn't safe to leap from the top of the toilet cubicle (a 6 foot drop to the floor), I knew she resented him blocking the sinks with the little towels all the children took into school with them; I would have resented it too. I know it was bad that he loved to make a flood (having used the little towels as makeshift plugs). I realised it was bad form to play with the light switches while she was out of the room. And I understood how difficult it must have been to explain to the little girl's mother how her daughter came to be some miniature mud-kip who had to be sent home in borrowed clothes.

I don't know if you've spotted the constant which links all these events together? Yes, besides mini-RT teen himself. I always used to wonder, where was the teacher when this was happening? I did make some noises to this effect when she told me, but was too young and nervous to ask her directly. Now I would speak out and say, in my best English battle-axe voice, 'And where were *you* at the time?'

It's not that I expected her to take responsibility for my son's misdemeanours, I really did think he was uniquely responsible for each one of them. But was it too much to ask for a class of 4-5 year olds to be supervised by someone, even if it wasn't their teacher? Also, I always came away with the impression that she would have much preferred teaching the older children - she had been moved down from the oldest class to the youngest. Perhaps with more mature children it's easier to 'nip out' of the classroom, or ignore it when they have elongated trips to the bathrooms.

My proudest day of mini-RT teen's inappropriate behaviour came when he stood up to the school bully. The child in question was well known for being a horrible bully who singled out the youngest children and would get them out of sight and properly hit them. This was a boy of 6 years old, so goodness knows what he was like in later life.

He looked forward to each new class coming up from Nursery into Reception. In Nursery they had a protected, separate playground. In Reception they joined the main school, who all shared the same areas. He chose children from Reception and picked and would hurt little girls as much as little boys. He was despicable.

Yes, the school knew about him but nothing was really done. The headmistress was the same one who had been my teacher when I was there and she didn't like any bad press for the school, so, rather than dealing with it out in the open, it was brushed under the carpet.

One day, the bully decided to pick on my son. As usual, mini-RT teen was doing something inappropriate: this day, he was swinging, monkey-style, on the metal bars on the ramp next to the school building. Curling himself up, he was spinning round on them in a way that would give health and safety people a panic attack.

Bully-boy saw him doing this and came to teach him a lesson, using the swinging as an excuse. He came up behind him and challenged him. I don't know what he said to my son as no one was close enough to hear and my son couldn't remember. It must have been pretty bad, whatever it was. My excitable, sociable, kind-hearted mini-RT teen swung off the bars, whipped round and charged the bully, head-butting him in the stomach.

At the end of the day, the teacher came out, as usual, to 'have a word'. This is the only time I saw a glimmer in her eye. She explained about the latest inappropriate behaviour and said she had told min-RT teen how it was unacceptable to be violent to people. She told me they were overlooking it this time as other children had stood up for him and said he was being bullied.

All of this was said with a twinkle in her eye and a softer tone to her voice. This slightly cold, humourless woman was barely concealing her delight at my son's actions. He had done what they as teachers were not allowed to do. She couldn't condone it but she could be pleased at the final comeuppance of the school bully.

This changed my son's notoriety in school, at least among the children. He was looked at with admiration and they were proud of him. I was proud of him too, even though I knew he had acted out of instinct and could never have inflicted harm on the bully if he had thought about it first.

The inappropriate behaviour, in society's terms, has continued. These days, RT teen is at college, doing his Art course. His behaviour is exemplary; in most ways he is a model student. Except that now, his mouth is inappropriate. No, I don't mean he curses and he isn't mean to people. What he does is Speak His Mind. He also speaks out for other people, in his own quiet way.

His tutor, a woman who is often at cross-purposes with him (no changes there, then), is fond of explaining things many times, to her 'special' students. I'm sure she is a woman of the best intentions and only explains things a lot because she thinks her students will understand it better that way. I don't know about the other 'specials', but as far as RT teen is concerned, as soon as he hears the repetition coming, he switches off.

One day, she asked him to show the other students how he had done something on the computer, as she was pleased with his work. She wanted him to explain the steps he had taken. So, the group gathered round and he started to explain. Except, like some aspies, he tends to hesitate before speaking - a non-verbal full stop between sentences. Each time he hesitated, his tutor jumped in and said what she thought he had been going to say.

After a few goes at speaking for himself, RT teen asked her, quietly, if she would come out of the room with him. Once in private, he explained, with suppressed fury, that he did not want her butting in, that every time she did it he lost track of what he was saying and what was the point of asking him to explain to the others if she was going to do it for him? She flinched and apologised. They returned and he carried on as he wanted, giving the group his undivided attention.

I know this is standing up for himself and, I must admit, I flinched a little myself at the anger it must have taken for him to speak to his tutor like this. But it's still counted as inappropriate in some way because it's seen as rude, or too forthright. I mean, the tutor should always be right and be respected and if the students are in the assisted learning programme, then her way is best, right?

I feel that RT teen should continue to be inappropriate. He has an inappropriate way of only ever seeing the person and never their looks, disability, or age. They are always a person first. Inappropriately, as far as assisted learning is concerned, he treats them just as he'd like to be treated himself and explains things in a quiet, demonstrative way that gets to the heart of the matter.

I don't know if he always explains things to them in a way all of them can understand. I do know that his soft voice, kind eyes and willingness to show rather than tell will probably have them listening to his every word.

I have mentioned inappropriate behaviours a lot today and I realise that the last examples, with RT teen at college, will seem very different from the little boy plastering his classmate with mud. It is different, as we all grow. As we get older, our behaviours change and so do our challenges. In the written and the spoken word, RT teen can still struggle to express himself, unless it's a subject he holds dear. But that means when he does express himself, he gets to the point and is honest.

I know there are many aspies out there who suffer from inappropriate honesty - I'm one of them. And this is often coupled with expressing yourself in a way that seems designed to cause offence. How can it be acceptable in a civilised society to speak to people in a direct, no-nonsense way that might hurt their feelings? Isn't it better to be subdued and kind instead?

I'm not sure. I've tried the subdued and kinder route and ended up gnashing at the furniture once I'm home. I've also tried inappropriate honesty (usually by accident) and then worried afterwards, but had a curiously satisfied feeling too.

When you are honest, brutally, genuinely, inappropriately honest, people will almost always flinch. If you happen to be that way with another aspie, they might gasp, then agree with you, then tell you something about yourself that you don't want to hear.

If it's obvious you meant nothing by it or it was an accident, then you're more likely to have it overlooked and be forgiven. If, like RT teen, you fully intended it but spoke in a soft voice, people are unnerved. They don't know how to deal with explicit honesty dealt out with a gentle voice. It clashes in their heads that you could say something uncomfortable to hear in a kind tone.

In my experience, you will always keep the friends you're meant to have and get along with people who would like you, no matter what. The ones who find such honesty too off-putting are probably already put off by your other little ways so there wouldn't be too much harm done there.

I also think that society as a whole is rather like the school system: we are meant to be semi-independent within it, while always obeying the rules. As adults, society will not run to our parents if there is trouble, but it will challenge us and expect the right kind of behaviour. If you separate this behaviour from obviously criminal acts, you have a social code that we're all meant to follow.

It may vary from country to country, but in general we are not meant to tell Mrs H that her dress has three night's worth of supper down the front or explain to Mr P that his breath smells like the cat slept on his tongue.

We are meant to fit in with the rule, the norm and be like everyone else so that society can function. There are large types of inappropriate behaviour which clash with this, such as stripping in the chippy or shouting down the street at other people's dogs. There are also smaller inappropriate behaviours, like brutal honesty and laughing at things no one else finds funny.

Well, there we are. I can safely say, most aspies are tilted to the wrong side of peculiar when it comes to complying with all the social rules. Sorry, that's how it is. Whether aspie or not, there's nothing you can really do about it.

What comes to me the most is, if we are faithfully honest, as much as possible, be it on purpose or by accident, people will relax more and forgive it, especially if it isn't meant unkindly. There may be a temporary taking aback, but we will feel much better in ourselves for being the full-on aspie who tells it like it is. In this instance, if no other, it pays to be inappropriate.

GIVING IT ALL AWAY

As aspies, sometimes we are accidentally open about ourselves, even when the last thing we would want to do is share what we are with others.

For years, I tried to hide the real me, beneath what I thought of as appropriate behaviour at the time or by putting myself across as nonchalant or expressionless. A lot of this was down to the school I went to, where any expression of emotion was an open door to bullies who jumped on it to make fun. By seeming uncaring or closed off, I was trying to protect myself, long after I left school behind.

These days, I often wonder what my face is doing while I'm not thinking about it. IT teen says I have a severe look sometimes, as if I am ready to give someone a real telling off or leap to the attack.

This is at times when I think I'm just wandering along, doing nothing in particular.

When I am actually annoyed, be it in a restaurant with bad service or someone deliberately goading me, well, it's lucky I don't have snakes for hair. I have the famous **Look**, which I usually don't know I've used until the waitress has flinched and stepped back or the small student suddenly finds their work much more interesting.

When I'm trying to be normal, I concentrate on my behaviour and facial expressions. I attempt what I think is a pleasant smile, then if I catch sight of myself in a mirror, I see the smile is mainly in the eyes and my years of self-protection are betraying me again.

When I am attempting something more formal, like making a complaint or speaking to someone in authority, strangely I can do that one. It's like a switch being flicked and I'm what I need to be. This is very useful, though I'm confused as to why it might work when the others do not? Perhaps years of moaning and having little respect for authority combine at the right time and give me the oomph I need?

The other night, I was coming out of the supermarket and trying not to laugh. I don't even know what was funny now, I think I'd been eavesdropping again. Whatever caused it, I left the shop, weighed down with my bags and a smile on my face. A woman coming in looked very serious and a little worried but when she saw me, she returned my smile and her face lifted. It was accidental on my part, a side effect of poor self control, but it was one of those moments when I saw what is possible, if we step outside ourselves.

There have been many moments, for me and probably for you too, where I have affected someone else's day in a small way without meaning to do anything. It's often in those unguarded moments when our real, true selves are at the front of everything that this happens.

The woman being cheered up by me smiling at her is a good example. It's a moment in life when I seemed to have reached out to someone else and they responded. This is always a shock to me as I am very nervous about reaching out to others, even if I know I am the 'strong' one in the situation. If you reach out, there is the danger that you won't be able to draw back again.

I think to myself, after these little moments, that the next time I'll smile anyway, whether or not it's for a different reason. What is the sense in going along, trying to protect yourself, when you do more harm than good? Why not open up a little and have that nice experience of interacting with other people in a good way?

Then life moves on and I forget again and I just hurry along, doing my best and hoping it'll all be okay, never really remembering my promise to be more open and let people in. It's very hard to remember or hang on to this kind of contradictory thinking, when your natural instinct is to be closed off, rather than wide open.

It feels like an open house phenomenon, where if you let one person bring a friend, you'll suddenly have hundreds of people turning up, drunk and expecting food. It sounds extreme to equate being more open to opening up every barrier within yourself, but that's actually how it feels.

A dam breaking, is what we expect if we let down our guard and invite people in. Harsh experience and firmly-held memories tell us that being open and guileless bring in the bad as well as the good. That those people we don't want to be with are the ones most likely to hurt us if we let everyone in.

More outgoing types will make some comment about it being worth it, taking the rough with the smooth, that you don't gain anything by keeping everyone at bay. They're right, of course, it's just that the rough hurts, that keeping people at bay feels safe and, when you've been wounded and are wondering where to go from here, it doesn't seem worth it.

You see, beneath every blank-faced aspie, looking like they drift through life without seeing anyone around them, there is a seething pot of emotions, often based on past experience. We are informed by past hurts and take them as advice for the future. We feel them keenly and don't want to be hurt that way again.

We are afraid that if you see the real person inside, you'll wonder what all the fuss was about and turn away.

After all, how many times have you smiled at a stranger and they don't respond? Or worse, looked away, in case you want to speak to them? Imagine this, on a much grander scale, as the aspie giving themselves to other people and finding they are unwanted.

I find the best way is to do what you can and be open when it feels possible. Smiling at strangers is a small risk, as practice makes their rejection less hurtful. Talking to people you meet is a good one, though brings it's own risks as the more you talk, the more aspie you become!

These days, fuelled with more self-knowledge than I've had in the past, I try to be more open. I try not to keep the barriers up all the time. Trying is what I can do and sometimes it works.

An all-out open house would not work; it would be a nightmare scenario where the real me is suddenly open to the world. How bad would that feel?

Hmm. The keener amongst you may have noticed the final, fatal flaw in that argument. You see, I may walk through the shop, blank-faced or stern, and I may only smile by accident at strangers, but each time I write this blog I am opening myself up fully and without compromise to the people reading it. I am doing the very thing I say I cannot in my everyday life.

There have been some hairy moments, some rough with the smooth but, like my outgoing friends, I can say it's been worth it. More than worth it! I can do on screen what I find so difficult in normal life; the written word, always my friend, giving me the power to open the door and let it all out.

There is a small twist to the tale, readers. Thanks to this blog, I am becoming more open in person too, whether people like it or not! I am more outspoken and outgoing than I was and, predictably, more obviously aspie as a result.

This is a good thing. I am being myself and if other people don't like it, well, I already showed them where the door was, didn't I? But as it turns out, no one has needed to use it yet.

I've become braver, if not fearless, thanks to giving it all away on here. Sooner or later, I will be doing the same in real life too. I can feel it bubbling up, ready to escape. I wonder if it will all happen at once, like it did with the blog, or if I'll be able to contain the aspie-ness enough, so that I don't scare the horses?

Who knows? But when it happens, I'll be sure to tell you everything, as usual, dear readers.

UNDER-ACHIEVING AND POTENTIAL

I've read many times that people with Aspergers tend not to fulfil their potential, that they under-achieve and actively avoid becoming the people their natural talents seem to want them to be.

Yes, I can see where that comes from and I don't want any angry parents writing in and telling me off for disagreeing with this view. I am the classic under-achiever, I have disappointed people in ways large and small and, guess what? I knew I was doing it.

Is that the hardest part for others to accept, I wonder? That the aspie knows they should be able to do more but, for whatever reason, shies away and retreats from their opportunities?

Perhaps, or could it be that we also sometimes suffer from our loved ones assuming that someone with our talents or intelligence must automatically be able to do certain things, as if that's the way of the world. That if we can't do them easily, we should learn to cope and still manage to become the person they thought we would.

Sorry, readers, but it doesn't always work that way in the aspie world. In fact, it never seems to go to plan, mainly because the plans are made by other people and not the aspie themselves. And for the aspie who does make plans and have ambitions for the future, have they factored in the effect their Aspergers may have on that future?

It's all quite complex, this issue of potential and under-achieving, made all the harder to sort out by each aspie having their own difficulties, which so often present as them being awkward rather than in need.

I have to tell you, it was a very great relief to me to know I was one of many aspies who found the same things difficult when it came to coping with life and trying to achieve to our full capabilities. In all cases, the main reason for failure was not working with the aspie side of life, in trying to step past it and pretend it wasn't there, or work through it, as if it was a moment of weakness.

Please read this chapter with a kindly eye on your own aspie's perceived failings. Try to see them in a new light. I hope you come away with a better understanding of how much we *do* achieve and how our potential is not a uniform thing, to be bottled and kept on a shelf, but a flowing, fluid creature which deserves to be free.

THE MYTH OF THE UNDER-ACHIEVER

Somewhere along the line it became normal to label aspergers as under-achievers. I don't want to beat about the bush on this one. I'm not planning to cover it in ivy and call it Art; this is a standard response which crops up again and again. Aspergers often equals under-achieving, a failure to fulfill potential. And, to be completely honest, I prove that point myself.

I have said before that I was an academic at school. I tried hard, enjoyed exams (a freak in more ways than one), I wanted to go out into the world and have a career, as well as getting my degree.

Alongside this I always wanted to be a writer. In fact, I always *was* a writer, the *being* a writer is just what happens when you get published. I wanted to spend my whole working life sharing the stories which rampaged through my head. But writing was a hobby, something you did in your spare time. The rest of your working life was the proper job. If you happened to become successful with the writing, then that could become the career - until then, it was delegated to the role of interloper, time-sucker, parlour trick.

In the defence of anyone who ever told me to get a proper job, I was also easily distracted, unlikely to knuckle down and write every single day, only producing full works when the inspiration carried me far enough. When it did carry me, then the magic happened, but I didn't have the necessary maturity to realise I had to write even when I didn't want to.

So, the under-achieving side of things had its claws in everywhere. In the writing, with my need to only get out the typewriter when the muse struck and in the jobs I did after I left school.

When I left sixth form, I knew I had to work. I wanted to, I was very keen to get out into the world (ignorance: bliss). It didn't take many days of having a proper job for me to realise I needed to go and finish my A levels and escape to college. It's amazing how much incentive you can gain from working at the bottom of the pay scale in a public-facing role.

In the two years between leaving school and going away to college, I managed to fit in four paid jobs and one voluntary one. Volunteering at Oxfam at the very start of my career was the one I liked the best, because the old ladies I worked with thought I was their pet teenager (I was), I liked it when they had fights and there was always tea and biscuits on offer. Also, they were pleased to see me every day.

The paid jobs followed a pattern which became familiar over the years. I would start a job and it was going to be perfect. You've no idea how perfect it was going to be. I was going to love it, they would love me, I would progress quickly and be the boss in record time. Etc. Except it never quite worked out like that.

My good intentions would be eroded by difficult days, monotony, malicious colleagues (not many of those but it only takes one), more monotony, routine and no escape when I was feeling delicate and needed to be alone. I would do my best and mostly it was good enough.

Then, over time, it would start to wear me down and the thought of going into work would become almost as painful as the work itself. It became difficult even to think about going in, until I couldn't stand it any longer and moved on to the next job.

So, despite my brains and my need for approval, I was still the under-achiever at work because I never lived up to my potential. If every day had been like my best days, or even my good days, there's no telling where I would be now. For certain, I would not be writing this blog. I'd be a high-powered business woman with a nanny and a gardener. I also wouldn't be writing my books about different worlds, a yearning for change, magic in everyday life and dogs as big as horses.

I loved college. Learning for its own sake, mixing with all kinds of clever, interesting and barmy people. Tutors who treated you like real people and who were more eccentric than me! Imagine that, a real-life tutor who made me seem almost normal, introducing me to the magic of religious philosophy. Francesca, if you are out there and reading this, the things you opened up to me are in every single book I write: thank you!

After college, the shadow of the proper job reared its head again and I slipped back into the under-achieving cycle. I did have some happy years as a stay-at-home mum - absolutely no under-achieving there! - and then back to work again.

It wasn't until I started working for myself that I realised what was wrong with all those jobs. Well, actually, not much was wrong with the jobs, it was me who wasn't right. Working for myself, I was able to structure my working days and take time off when I needed to recuperate from the world. If things became too stressful, I didn't need to quit and move on, I just needed to take time out. Knowing you have this release valve is often enough for you to hardly ever need to use it. It's the perspective that matters.

From there, I followed the path which led me here, to you. I learned enough about myself to look back over my patchwork CV and realise what had been going wrong and why. I was able to look back and see that I would have been unsuitable for any job that added stress to my life, without an acceptable Exit signposted into the plan.

And this is where I need to come back to the theory of the under-achieving aspie. This is the point where I say *@?$&X*! to it. Yes, you heard me, I said *@?$&X*! and I meant it!

Aspies do not under-achieve: everything they do is an achievement. I don't mean that to sound patronising, I'm being genuine. Let me show you.

On the outside, when I arrive slightly late for work, looking disheveled, I have been under-achieving again. I am more than capable of being on time, of organising myself and presenting myself in an appropriate manner. There are people at work with me who have far greater burdens in life and who arrive with a cheerful smile and immaculate hair.

Now, let's take another look.

I was awake half the night, thinking about coming in. The stress has built to a point where I feel physical pain when I think about it. When I sit watching TV with my family, part of me is still at work. When I talk to people about other things, I'm thinking about work.

When I do the washing and there are work clothes in it, I feel that muddy pit in the bottom of my stomach curdle as I anticipate having to wear them again.

When I washed my hair last night, I forgot to dry it properly because I had to get my clothes ready for work today. I was feeling upset and trapped, so I sat with my family for longer than normal and went to bed late. Then when I couldn't sleep, I thought of what I could do today, instead of being at work. And I yearned for that other life.

When I woke this morning, I was mentally exhausted. I should have been on time but I couldn't focus because I knew I was coming in here, instead of staying at home, where it's safe.

I need to be safe right now. I need to be away from here. I fantasise about leaving at lunchtime and never coming back, I get a lift from that image of me walking out of the door, away from the flickering neon lights and the need to be happy and cheerful and always as people expect me to be.

I know my colleague has a greater burden than me and I admire her. I also know that, for her, work is a release and she heals by being there, just like I would heal if I went home.

I didn't under-achieve when I went to work, I did what I could with what I have. I made the best of it and, when I could stand no more, I left. When I had recovered and felt healthy again, I applied for another job and the cycle repeated itself. Some jobs lasted longer than others, often thanks to the good people I met while working there, the sort of people who, just by being themselves, are a healing, restorative force.

Please, though, don't use the words 'under-achiever'. For an aspie at school, with brains to spare and an ability to work for hours on end on something they love, it is not under-achieving when they can't cope with homework, school, the people, the noise, the smells, jostling in the corridors and the light as it streams through the windows, inviting them out into the clear, clean, loving day, away from everything harsh and unreal.

For the aspie at work, they don't under-achieve when they get things wrong after doing it right a hundred times, or for snapping at people or using the wrong words, or turning up late. It isn't good working practice, but neither is it under-achieving. It doesn't matter what they can do or what they're capable of; today they are only capable of turning up and being here, and that was with a force of will that was practically used up when they made it out of the house.

For the aspie who could have had a career, but prefers a quiet, low paid job with part-time hours and spends the rest of their time doing something pointless that doesn't bring in any money. They are definitely not the under-achiever: they are the wise one who discovered the key to success. They earn enough money to get by and spend the rest of their time doing what they love. They know the value of time and life, because they have found out how to combine what is necessary with what they are capable of maintaining.

And my last word would be for the small child, just starting out in their school career. They will most likely be displaying the more active face of aspergers, where it can present like attention deficit disorder. They will be cantering around the playground, accidentally pushing people, behaving badly, being naughty and loud and forgetting to stop all that once they're back in the classroom.

They can achieve more, they can work when they want to and they can't tell you why they do it. They don't under-achieve either, what they are doing is rushing at life to see if it will back down. They are shouting, here I am! and waiting to see what shouts back. They still have their enthusiasm for the new and unknown, they still want to learn all there is to know.

Their only under-achievement is in not being able to carry that enthusiasm forward through their lives, without losing self-esteem or becoming too tender on the inside. And even that isn't an under-achievement, it's a by-product of being different in a world which only values differences it can understand.

The next time anyone uses the words *potential* and *achievement* in relation to your aspie, imagine that small child, mouth wide open in a joyful battle cry, eyes bright as they survey the crowded playground, looking for their next big adventure.

That's where we all wish to be, in that moment of shining pleasure, the wind blowing, the sky clear and the doors wide open to the day.

PRESSURE, PRESSURE, PRESSURE

Okay, I'm going to mention the 'P' word again...yes, Pressure. Also, Stress and Responsibility, as I've come to realise those two party-poopers are just the bodyguards for Pressure, who is always the main problem.

Now, for those of you who have mulled this one over, usually late at night or at one of those awkward moments when you have a sudden epiphany in a crowded place, yes, I realise that you can also argue that pressure is secondary to stress and responsibility; that it's better to say pressure is the feeling you get when the other two are dancing up and down on your head.

That's the way I thought of it too, and there is some truth in it. Rather like a woven blanket, it can be hard to see where one thread ends and another begins. Is it even worth trying to separate them, as they're so closely bound together? I believe it is and I'll tell you why.

I've spent many years trying to face up to responsibility and struggling to recognise stress when it was affecting me. Stress can be so tenuous and misleading that you tend to think it's just life having a kick at you, not that it's a thing which exists by itself. Isn't it logical to say that stress is always caused by something? I used to follow that thought to a place where I could blame myself for not bearing up under life's responsibilities and so making myself stressed, just because I couldn't cope.

Responsibilities, those creatures other people seem to take in their stride, have always reared and bit for me. Give me a sour dog or a scary pony any day over a mean-spirited, uncompromising, aggressive responsibility. I've tried the various ways to cope with them, for without responsibility you may as well give up all hope of living a normal life. There is always something that you need to be responsible for, even if it's just making sure you eat every day or pay the water bill.

Stress, when I could see it, was a horrible, sneaky feeling that I never saw right in front of me. Many times it has been up to other people to ask me if I'm stressed, or to tell me I am, then prove it by giving me examples of things I've done or said that show it. I really appreciate that kind of approach because I've never been able to get a good look at stress or recognise it for what it was. I've become afraid of it, like it's a very patient assassin, willing to bide its time while I go on, oblivious, trying to deal with everything.

I now have a great way of finding out if I'm stressed, though I certainly wouldn't recommend it. I suffer from what I fondly call my Victorian throat. No, I don't have an overwhelming need to wear high lace collars, or tie ribbons around my neck. It's that feeling you get when it's like you have something stuck in your throat, making it a little difficult to swallow. The Victorians called it globus hystericus, linking it to a nervous disposition. Nowadays it is recognised as having physical causes separate from any emotional or psychological ones, but I'm an old-fashioned girl and mine is caused by anxiety.

The above is a long-winded way of explaining that stress is much less able to creep up on me these days because I now have my Victorian throat to warn me. I will be having what I think of as a mostly normal day and then, ba-boo! there it is, that familiar clogged feeling in the throat. I'll think, 'Oh, am I stressed then?' Invariably, no matter how surprised I am, if I pick my way back through the events of that day or the one before, I can see where things have become difficult and understand why I might be stressed. So, useful but annoying.

Now, back to pressure: why do I think it's the main man, the one that stress and responsibility protect? Simply put, pressure is the root of all stress, because without a feeling of pressure, caused by outside influences or inner emotions, there would be no stress. If we were able to float through life, letting all worries wash over us, we would feel no pressure to behave a certain way or feel this instead of that; so, we would feel no stress either.

As for responsibility, yes, this one does exist outside of stress or pressure. Responsibilities are independent of many things in life, but, they still exist to protect pressure. In fact, you could almost say they are the children of pressure, because if we had nothing to do, nothing to be responsible for, then there would be no pressure in the first place.

Pressure can be viewed as drive, ambition, hope, aspiration, the need for change or to prove oneself. All of these thoughts, feelings and ideas are accompanied by pressure, as without it, each one of them is like a will o' the wisp, floating off into the trees, untouched and never properly seen.

It would be true to say that some form of pressure is at the very root of all human existence. We need to survive, we push ourselves to do what we must to make that happen. Move on to the more complex, modern world and this need to survive is blended and distorted by all the other needs jostling for attention. Some are more essential than others, but they are all caused by that inner drive to become more than a piece of some yucky, primeval pond-scum floating across the face of early Earth.

Yes, there's the truth of it, readers: to be melodramatic about it, without pressure, we would be nothing. We would vegetate and wither, there would be no point to us.

Unfortunately, aspies have developed a finely-tuned sense for pressure and are more affected by it than the other evolved pond-scum (apologies to anyone who imagined themselves sprouting from an early flower). Aspies may not be able to recognise stress when it walks in the room, but they can sense pressure entering the country at the nearest port.

It's as if there is some kind of booby-trapped defence system at work, one that is set up just for pressure and is able to ignore all the others. Perhaps aspies recognise pressure as that instigator of so many other problems, so always make sure they know when it's coming?

Stress can float in, cause havoc and leave the aspie reeling or punching the carpet and screaming. Responsibilities can give the aspie super-powers and, where you thought you had an aspie, you actually have some anime-style blur of colour as the aspie zooms off into the distance.

Pressure, on the other hand, sets off every early-warning system in the aspie's arsenal. They don't need super powers to see it coming - pressure-detection *is* the super power. They can feel it as it moves across the land, they can hear it's grey, monotone timbre as it whispers to itself, they can see the edge of the toe as it creeps up to the door.

All of this, all of it, readers, is *terrifying*. There may be early-warning systems, there may be super powers of detection, but **there is nowhere to hide**! Nothing can be done in the face of pressure, there is no escape. Panic ensues, utter panic and life falls apart, again.

And this is why we avoid pressure at all costs. What we want to avoid is that feeling of panic and helplessness, in the face of pressure which by-passed all our systems and came right into the room with us. We remember the feeling of fear and the knowledge we were powerless and we'll do just about anything to avoid feeling like that again.

This is why pressure is the main problem. Readers, forget stress and responsibility, they are not where you should be looking. Stretch your neck to see past them and you'll just be able to make out a grey figure in the distance. Is it moving closer? It's almost impossible to tell. Like the moving hands of a clock, it comes, slowly, methodically, drawing near. But then, when least wanted, it can cover any distance and be right by your side.

I can't offer a solution to this as there really isn't one. I offer it as some explanation as to why the aspie mind abhors pressure above all things - and why all things come to be about pressure. I also offer it as some solace to the best beloveds who have to pick up the pieces after pressure comes calling. It may have seemed incomprehensible that your aspie should have had such a reaction to the x, y or z of life when it was all fine in the end and nothing happened. Here we have the reason why: this time it was fine, maybe last time it was too, but some times it isn't fine and pressure is there before we know it, making it all go so wrong.

Readers, chin up and carry on in the face of this constant threat. You know you forget all about pressure for long stretches at a time. You know that when pressure is near it seems as if it's always been there and always will be. The truth of life falls somewhere in between and life must be lived, after all.

We cannot bow to pressure more than necessary. All we can do is look out for the appearance of the bodyguards and listen to our early-warning systems, so we know when pressure is close by.

To aspies and non-aspies, I would give you one final piece of advice: listen to those feelings and take no notice of what *should* be. If pressure is felt then it will cause a reaction - there's no point explaining it away and expecting everything to be all right. A feeling is real and the reaction is real. Just hold on and help it to pass, without judgement or criticism.

And to pressure: I know you now and you'll not get near me without a fight, because I have bodyguards of my own. The grey, monotone, relentless feelings will always be defeated by understanding and loving yourself. I promise.

SEPARATE, DETACH AND ESCAPE

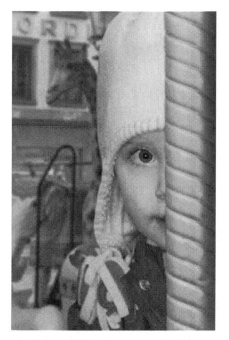

I remember watching a TV programme when I was younger. One of the characters was having a bad day and had decided to stay under a blanket until they could face coming out. This was hilarity indeed and much of the episode was spent gaining laughs at the expense of the peculiar and stubborn person under the blanket, who if I remember it right, only showed their face near the end of the show.

Various attempts were made to bring them out. Talking, pretending sympathy, poking them, taunting them, laughing and, finally, trying to whip the blanket away from them. All of this was played for laughs and the blanket-hider was shown to be unreasonable and completely over-reacting. Everyone else was reasonable, even when they were goading their friend. They knew the person was having a bad time, but you can't make anything better by staying under a blanket, can you?

I remember watching it and thinking how nice and dark it would be under that blanket. How you could probably ignore the people outside it, even if they were laughing and shouting, because your safe place would still be safe. The only time I was really perturbed was when they wanted to take the blanket away from him - that I didn't like.

He does emerge, of course. He comes out, blinking and bleary-eyed, looking down in the mouth but more or less back to normal. Life continues, jokes move on, he is okay again.

Like I've said before, things I watch on TV or in the movies, stay with me in a way real life doesn't. The image of hiding under a blanket was tucked away in a soft corner of my mind and would come back out many times as the years passed. I often thought of sitting in my bed, the blanket over my head.

A bit like when you're a child and you build a den out of sheets and blankets. It doesn't matter where it is, in the garden or the middle of the living room: once you're inside, it's a safe place, shut off from the real world and it's all yours.

The implicit rules of any den are that it belongs to the person who built it, others can only enter with permission and the child who pulls it apart is often a complete rogue in the making and will come to no good.

That is the blanket, then. A re-branding of the childhood den, a place to revert to, a safe place no one can enter without permission. Somewhere you can be alone if you need to be, the outside world kept at bay, not by a thin layer of material, but by the invisible force which surrounds any imaginary barrier. It is safe because you *feel* it is.

So, what do you do when you're not a child anymore and you don't have the option to physically hide under a blanket? What happens if you need to be in the safe place and you're somewhere completely open and public? This is where it all depends on your coping mechanisms.

As adults, we are usually able to behave in a certain way. We may feel like screaming in the middle of the supermarket, but we rarely do. We may feel like running out of there, pushing aside trollies and ripping tins off the shelves as we go. We rarely do that either. Sometimes we do end up shouting, or making explosive noises which we didn't realise were on their way out until - pop! - there they were.

No, unfortunately, as adults, most of us have learned to obey the rules of civilised society. It may be better for our mental and emotional health to run screaming from the store. And I'm certain it would be good for us to fling things off the shelves on the way past - I have always wanted to do that! But we're not allowed.

What we do, instead, is leave as soon as possible. Sometimes we'll feel better by the time we can leave, the moment will have passed and we are sane human beings again. Sometimes you have a full day of responsibilities ahead of you that just cannot be ignored. There's no screaming and running from those either.

So, you plod on. And on, and on. You do this and that and cope with this and that, and all the while you are still partly in that moment, in the middle of the store, where your mind said **Leave Now** and you ignored it.

Eventually, you will reach a quieter part of the day. Home at last, feet up, kettle on, worries and stresses shelved once more. Except, they're not. You might feel better to be home and away from everything, but your worries and stresses follow you. Remember, you still didn't get to scream and run, did you? That means you have unfinished business.

That evening you may feel a little stressed or angry about nothing in particular. You might think to yourself, I'm glad to see the back of today. You can probably do whatever else you needed to do before going to bed.

That night, there's a good chance you'll sleep. It might not be a night of lying in your bed, glaring at the mental image of yourself. In the morning, though, you'll be exhausted. That's because you still have that unfinished business hanging over you and it *is* exhausting, holding up all that weight by yourself.

This is one of those moments where the safe and secure blanket idea comes into play. Today you may have as many stresses and responsibilities as yesterday. You still have to face them and you tell yourself it will be okay, you've had some rest in between. Today is a new day, you say to yourself.

This is another point where it all comes down to your coping mechanisms: some people will get up and do it all again, others will hear the creaking of the Off switch and stay where they are.

Fast forward for the people who managed to get out of bed and go through it again. Fast forward another evening trying to convince themselves it's all fine. And you're still back to another morning, feeling like the World is not outside, but *inside*, beating down the door of your bedroom, hungry eyes searching for you, even before you wake.

There comes a point where your unfinished business comes to roost, settling on you with a weight you didn't expect and cannot cope with. There is a stage for all of us, aspie or not, where it simply doesn't matter what other things you have to do: you must not do it today.

Physically, mentally, emotionally, this is a blanket day. This is a time when it wouldn't matter if your room was full of people who loved you, coaxing you out; you wouldn't come. This is a tight, no-manoeuvre predicament and there is only one way to deal with it.

That's because, sooner or later, those moments when you feel like screaming and running away, they come back and in full force.

You need to step back and step out, stay at home or go out - do whatever it is that makes you feel safe.

Take your blanket moment, push everything else to one side. Be like the character in the TV show and ignore what anyone says or does to persuade you you're being unreasonable, irrational, irresponsible. You may disappoint others, let them down, upset them or even anger them. Sorry people, this is not about you, this is about someone with aspergers who, if they don't have their time out, will not be the same person tomorrow that they were yesterday.

Take it and hold it tight, your hour or day of a safe place. Make it count. If you stay at home, unplug the phone and do whatever you like, as long as it doesn't cause you stress. If you go out, enjoy the open freedom, the feeling of being able to get away and escape.

Bottle it, my friend and keep it in its own safe place, inside you, for the next time you feel stressed and can't do anything about it. Picture it, remember it, have it ready in your mind and touch it gently when you need comfort. Visualise these moments of being apart and separate from everything that bothers you.

This is my way of coping in the sad times when I wouldn't need a grappling hook to scale tall buildings, or when it means nothing to me how the other person thinks or feels, I only need to push them aside and get away. Within me I try to keep the treasured moments, stored up like wood for winter, where I have been able to choose freedom and its' deep, calming breaths.

And at the other end of that safe time, with your real or imaginary blanket, you'll also be like the TV character when you emerge:

you will be bleary-eyed and confused, because you were so apart from the world and so within your own space, you forgot for a moment how confusing it could all be. It may take a little time to get back into the swing of things and be able to go through the supermarket without needing to scream.

You will get back into it. I promise that, as long as you can take yourself to your safe place and time when you need to be there, you will be able to come back and cope with life again. Maybe not so well as you would like, though, because needing to be safe in such a strong and definite way is a sure sign something is not right with your life. If you need to escape to the point of being unable to function without it, look again at what led up to it and see what you can change.

Whatever you do, don't reach the stage where the blanket moment envelopes you unawares, and you collapse from the pressure of not having saved yourself sooner. What you need to do is find some balance between this total collapse and running out of the shop, screaming your head off.

However, if I do hear the sound of footsteps hurtling towards me and the sound of a long, joyous scream bouncing off the aisles, I won't be afraid. I'll know it's just you, on your way into the sunshine. just please, try not to toss me into the apples on your way past.

HOW ASPERGERS PRESENTS ITSELF

I feel I make Aspergers sound like it dresses itself in front of the mirror, then struts down the street, waiting for people to notice it. And yet, this is very far from the truth because Aspergers is a secretive, shy creature that hides behind anything it can find and only comes out into the full light by accident or when carried along on a wave of enthusiasm.

Aspergers is such an awkward thing, you see. When you want people to know about it, you often can't find the words to explain. When you 'misbehave', such as accidentally insulting someone by pointing out the obvious, it looks like you're back-tracking when you blame the Aspergers. If you look back at a situation and try to explain that your Aspergers was at work there, it can still be difficult because you can't remember exactly *how* it was at work and what happened at the time.

Added to this all the times when you were able to go through life without Aspergers getting in the way, or you were having a really good day and achieved great things. Non-aspies then expect consistency, you see, and if you managed something once they expect you to manage it again.

This is where the difficulties lie, as being an aspie is not about consistency, unless you count the reliable nature of never being anything but an aspie. Sometimes we manage things and sometimes we don't, but we are still the same person. And most of the time, we couldn't tell you why it worked today but might not work tomorrow.

So much has to be taken on trust and this is where the family and friends of the aspie come into their own. If they can show that support and trust and kindness, even when it seems incomprehensible that the aspie is falling apart over such little things, then the next time it may be easier.

Aspies have problems remembering all the myriad of life's details but they never forget how they felt. Feelings have their own special memory port in the aspie brain and if you, as their best beloved, can make them feel safe and loved, it will never be forgotten.

ASPERGERS, THE SUBTLE DISABILITY

I admit it, I was going to title this one the *sneaky* disability, rather than subtle, but I didn't want people thinking aspies were sneaks. Some of us probably are sneaks, I don't suppose there is any reason to suppose we are all saintly little creatures who never put a foot wrong. But that's not quite what I mean.

I'm sure I'm not the only one who has made bad decisions because of aspergers. In fact, I could very probably say, we have *all*

made bad decisions because of aspergers. It's part of the scenery. Decision-making or pretending to decide and then rushing in, it's what makes aspergers such a creative way to live. Even those aspies who prefer to hole up at home, in the lovely light of the computer screen, will have been prone to this decision-making process.

You see, aspergers lets us think it belongs to us, as something we can see and almost touch. We know it's there, we can feel it looking from the edge of the door. It's all the way in the room with us when we open our big mouths and land ourselves in it again. Aspergers can be like some large pet, following us around, always ready to make it obvious who it belongs to when trouble ensues.

The notion of aspergers belonging to us is reinforced by those times, as in the part-time disability post, when we can pass for normal. Those times in life when you feel you can cope with things, you can act like a grown up for a change and none of your thought processes are dangling off the aspie cliff.

I guess I can sum it up by saying that while we may always identify ourselves as aspies, the aspergers itself can feel sporadic. One day we may stagger through our routines with the weight of the world on our shoulders; another day we can climb every mountain etc.

So, it's tempting to view aspergers as an on-off disability, one that allows us to get the job but not keep it, for instance. And this is where we have the big sillies, people, because none of that is true.

It's true to say we are always aspies. Sometimes, we are aspies who can manage anything and everything, but are you sure that isn't just because you had enough sleep or ate too much sugar or are going through a manic phase when the whole world can be yours?

Sometimes we can speak our mind and explain ourselves without aspergers getting in the way and tripping us up. It can feel like a triumph - we have beaten aspergers or managed to speak while it was looking the other way. Hmm. It's a nice thought but not true either. We have done these things and yay to us! But it's more likely the wind inside the mind was already blowing that way and gave us the extra push towards full expression.

I can corroborate this one as I was always a meek aspie, rarely speaking my mind, unless my mind spoke for me. As I've got older and gained more understanding of myself and the world in general, I have become more likely to speak my mind and not be meek. These days, if I keep my mouth shut, it's usually because I have decided to and not because I dare not speak. Another yay.

So, if we recognise that aspergers is here all the time, that we just react differently sometimes, due to many variables, what do I mean about it being a sneaky disability? Sorry, a *subtle* disability (sorry, aspergers, I love ya really).

I'm talking about those times when you acted, reacted, behaved or misbehaved in a way totally unrelated to aspergers. The times when you were the aspie but aspergers itself had been pushed to the background and you found yourself able to cope without mishap.

I mean those times when you have clarity of thought and speech and deed, when you could run the country if they let you, or at least hold down a steady job. Not the times when you feel manic, or so depressed everything seems clear because you've stripped all the goodness away. Those times when it all seems stable and you just happen to be able to do it.

You know what, I've had many times like that and I've lived normally for a little while; I've made decisions and accomplished things and, I admit it, wondered if this was what it was like to be normal.

Then, later, sometimes years later, I'll look back and realise aspergers was there all along; I just couldn't see it.

I'll give you an example. When I needed to go back to work the first time, I had reached the stage of being absolutely desperate for money. I was also passing through a very creative phase and had started a new book. It was going extremely well, but however good it was, I needed money.

At the same time as applying for jobs, I contacted agents about the book before it was finished. When I got the job offer, I also had a couple of positive responses about the book, one of which wanted to read the whole thing. But I didn't have the whole thing! Instead of replying and telling them this, I ignored the letter, feeling if they was positive, then later, once the book was finished, other people would be positive too. I took the full-time job and the book was never finished.

At the time, readers, I was well aware that I was choosing the job over the book - or over the writing as a whole. I felt I was making a sensible decision, given my finances and the fact I was a single mother. It was the only decision, I needed the money.

I had the idea that the writing would always be there, ready to be picked up when I was coping with my new work. It would still happen, everything would be fine. I just needed to get some money now and lift things up.

The trouble is, aspies sometimes can't cope with going to the corner shop, so I don't know how many of us could cope with a stressful full-time job as well as trying to write and run a household.

Now, I'm not saying I should have made a different decision. I still see that I had little choice. But looking back I still regret that book not being written. It had the glimmer about it, the magic of something which was able to write itself.

What I should have done was write back to the agent and explain. She may have lost interest, but who knows? That's one thing I could have done differently. Another is, I could have looked at part-time work. I was fixed on full-time because of needing the money. I also had the idea that I should return to full-time work because that's what real and proper people do in a normal life. Going part-time was always half measures, right? Real people do full-time and have mortgages and need to buy suits and stuff.

Yes, there are things that I could have done differently but I was convinced I was making rational, grown up decisions. I didn't know about aspergers then, so I couldn't take it into account - but I did know I found things hard to cope with. That couldn't matter though. Lots of people find life hard, we just have to man up and do it anyway.

So, where was the aspergers in this? Very definitely in my head-in-the-sand reaction to the agent asking for the full book. I even recognised that as 'cowardly' at the time (I was very fond of calling myself a coward back then).

Putting that aside, the rest was an adult decision-making process, with no bearing on aspergers, don't you think? I was facing my responsibilities and doing what needed to be done for the good of me and my family.

Except, what I was actually doing was ignoring any downsides and pushing myself to become the person I needed to be. I was shaping myself to fit, like so many aspies do. I was sure if I tried hard enough, I could be this full-time worker who coped with normal things.

As I needed to be that person, I made decisions based on what that type of person could do. I pretended to be her in the interviews, I tried to pretend to be her in the job itself. I bought the clothes and had my hair done. I re-scheduled our lives around it and wept tears over not being able to collect my children from school.

I slowly drizzled away, not coping with the imposed personality or lifestyle. It didn't work. With what I had chosen, it was never going to work, I just didn't realise it then.

The aspergers was always there, informing my decisions like background music lends atmosphere to a film. Even though I couldn't see it then or take account of it, I was behaving as a true aspie - creating a world to fit what I thought I needed or wanted. Any decisions made within this premise are bound to be faulty, however impeccable they seem, because at the very heart of it, we're not being true to ourselves.

Even now, when I can look aspergers in the face, I still get caught out on a regular basis. I can think I'm taking account of it, but I end up making decisions based on what I think should be instead of what is.

This is where aspergers is sneaky, you see. It's a very good mimic and can look at the world of other people and see where we are lacking. We can see what we're meant to do, compared to everyone else. If we accept we can't do it, then that's fine for a while, until we move onto a different scenario and decide we can do that instead.

The problem is, the different scenario often isn't very different at all. A good analogy would be all the jobs we work through. This job will be better than the last one because the hours are less. This one will be better because it's easier. I was so bored at the last one, this one will be better because it's more challenging.

Each time we swap the job, the aspergers is in full control, even though we've made the decisions based on good reasons. What we are doing is moving the scenery to suit our view that we should be doing this instead of that. As long as the scenery keeps changing then the situation is different and we can trust our decisions are objective.

Unfortunately, it just doesn't work that way. What we end up doing is moving our lives around while forgetting the one thing that doesn't change - ourselves. If you are the main character in the play, it really doesn't matter what the scenery looks like or how the lines change: you will be that character in the end and your actions will eventually match your personality.

And this is where I have to drop the big drama bomb. Aspergers is not our pet, our possession or even our disability. It is part of us. Not like a dart that has been fired into your behind, or a needle pushed under the skin to administer a steady dose of aspie-ness. Not like carrying a baby or having an ingrowing toenail. And not like having a split personality (though it often feels that way).

The shocker is, that aspergers is woven into the very fabric of our being, so that you cannot tell where it ends and where we begin. That's because aspergers is a name used to describe a set of behaviours that have things in common. It's a short cut. The very essence of being on the spectrum, of having a 'rainbow disability', is that we are all different.

Don't feel bad that aspergers is at the very heart of you, because all I'm doing is telling you that your aspie-ness is a part of you, not some alien, unfriendly thing. You are you and no one else will be an aspie in the same way. We can speak a lot of the same languages and relate many misadventures, but none of us is the same.

Aspergers is the subtle disability because it is so deeply bound to our real selves that we could never tease it free - and nor should we.

Everything we do and say is linked to being an aspie; it's a fact of life. I'm not saying don't trust yourself or always shy away from decisions. Better to go on in the best way you can and, when it comes to making a decision, view aspergers as a dear friend who is always with you. You're in this together so, as you move through life, remember to turn to aspergers and say, 'What do *you* think? Shall we?'

The funny thing about this subtle, sneaky disability is that it only wants to be heard and taken into account. Once you do that, the sneakiness and subtlety fall away and aspergers brightens, full of relief and hope for the future. If you work together with your aspergers, you can move mountains after all. And best of all, you can do it in the right way for you.

WHY CAN'T YOU DO IT?...
EXPLAINING ASPERGERS TO
FRIENDS AND FAMILY

I was trying to explain to IT teen last night why I couldn't go out and get full-time work. He said that with my CV I could be earning mega-money. I would only have to stick it for a few months and build up some cash, then I could do what I liked again (translate to 'whatever it is you do when you say you're working').

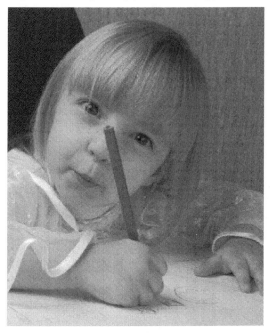

I pointed out that my CV was lovely, but had giant holes in it, or lots of little holes where I had started and finished lots of little jobs. He waved a hand and said that could be glossed over, I don't need to tell them *everything*. Yes, he knows me well - how many of us, when job hunting, tell them everything?

He pointed out how much money I made years ago when I did 'that full-time job' - fill in details of the job I mention as being the catalyst for finding out I couldn't cope with normal life and was the real beginning of my aspie journey.

This was something I'd covered before. I've occasionally tried to explain to IT teen, and other friends and family, why full-time 'proper' jobs don't work for me. I can explain it to *you*, readers. It comes out fine then. When I try explaining it in real life, with spoken words and expressions, to people who know me well, can you guess how it comes out?

"I can't do full-time work."

Sounds lame, doesn't it? Usually followed by the person asking why not. So, when IT teen asked the usual question, I wracked my brains. For a second I saw these blogs floating before me, I remembered how well it can be explained on here and I tried to summarise it for him.

"I just can't cope with it."

Yes, lame again. Followed by, 'it's the routine, the people, the stress' and so on. Cue raised eyebrows and snorts of disbelief (he is a teen, after all) and the comment that surely doing the same thing every day is easy??

You know, doing the same thing every day can be easy, especially when it's something you've chosen to do, like your routines at home. But I've found that doing the same things every day in a job sends me batty. It becomes part of the drudgery and stress and nearly always contributes to me leaving.

I tried to explain this and told him the only exception was when I worked at Tesco, as a personal shopper. I had to choose items from the shelves, match them to the computer and pack them in the boxes. Readers, that was wonderfully repetitive! It was so relaxing! Kind of like a real-life computer game. Plus, it was very, very early in the morning and I wasn't expected to talk to staff or customers.

I gave up this small oasis of tranquillity to go to work at the doctor's office, very busy and with constant staff and customer contact. I wouldn't make the same mistake again.

Unfortunately, bringing up the Tesco job did nothing for my credibility with IT teen. I had broken my own logic in avoiding doing the same thing every day by quoting a job when I did just that. I was also telling him that one of the most basic jobs I had ever done was one I enjoyed, and this was while he was trying to convince me to fulfil my potential and get a fabulous new job that would pay lots of money! You can see why he was exasperated.

As usual, I gave up trying to explain things to him. I know he meant no harm, he wants me to be able to do a job that uses my skills in a way that actually makes real money. Being self-employed is great when it comes to organising your life and using your skills, but as an aspie who always needs to keep an eye on the pressure-meter, I'm not likely to make big money anytime soon.

I could have explained more. I could have threatened him with no internet and made him read the blogs. I could have sat him down and read out the blogs to him (I'm becoming more cruel by the minute here). Yes, I could have rammed home the fact his mother is not like other mothers and reminded us both that I haven't turned out as expected.

I didn't do any of that. I guess at the bottom of it, you have to decide when and who you want to explain things to. As I've said, I have tried explaining to him before, but it's a drip-drip process. He knows his mother isn't like others, I don't want to emphasise that. I'm not ashamed of who I am but I am sometimes ashamed of how it's pushed me to live a life that is okay for me but perhaps isn't the best way to finance and support a household with children in it.

Yes, some of you may have spotted that I'm circling a familiar word here: Failure. I didn't want to explain fully as it does sound lame to a hale and hearty teenage boy. I didn't want to remind us both that I failed to become the person I expected to be and failed to create a well-off, balanced home where the socks always match and you don't have to panic-buy the packed lunch before school.

I avoided all of this because I need me and my children to be reminded of the home we *did* create: somewhere full of ideas, conversations, laughter, love, understanding of differences, night-time trips to spot meteors, day-time trips to the beach in the wild, windy Winter.

I want my children to remember that I worked for myself, around them and my other commitments, that I chose the home life over the career. Perhaps it was more a case of it choosing me, as I couldn't have coped with the career, but it created a new kind of life for all of us, where people and activities became more important than what was expected in a normal world.

So, when it comes to explanations, I try to keep it brief. I want my son to understand me, but I also need him to be a teenager, a dismissive, occasionally selfish creature that sees the world in clear lines with straightforward answers. There's time enough in the rest of life to see all the shades of grey that make up our world, our lives, our personalities.

I'm just hoping that the next time he brings up my CV, or a new job, or proper money, that I can remember more of my blogs than, 'I can't manage full-time work,' because, as much as I don't want to burden him with the full explanation, I would also like him to see the sub-text behind my words.

I guess what I could say is:

"I chose this life because it brought us all together."

It's so often the case that the explanation we offer fails to explain anything important. Perhaps we need to concentrate on emphasising the choices we make, rather than the ones we avoid. We should talk about choosing, not failing. We didn't choose to have aspergers, but we can choose to live creatively, in the glow of our differences, doing what we can to make it all work.

DOING WHAT NORMAL PEOPLE DO...

It strikes me that I should be in bed instead of writing this blog post, but as I was having a moan to my friend, I realised that the moan I was moaning was actually turning into my next blog post. Perhaps this is what happens when you blog about fundamental aspects of your life? Every moan is a potential blog and every blog is a little bit of a moan?

The moan in this case is the way that today seems to have been one thing after another, without room to breathe. When I examine it carefully, it hasn't really been like that, it just *feels* like it has. And the reason it has felt that way is because I needed time to recover from yesterday, but didn't get it.

So, working backwards, my moaning, occasional ranting and the innate feeling I have that I've turned into a piece of thin leather, fit only for patching a pair of old jeans, can all be traced to yesterday evening, when I went to a jewellery-making workshop.

I was very much looking forward to the workshop. I have a frustrated artist hiding within me who makes frequent, ill-judged attempts to escape and create masterpieces. I have the perfect vision inside my head of how the latest masterpiece will look, then when I'm finished it always, always looks like an angry five year old did it.

I can't sew, paint, draw, make curtains or patch that old leather onto the jeans. I can do cross stitch for some reason, but I think that's just Nature having a sense of humour with me. My practical talents are much like my artistic ones - if it requires artistic abilities, do not ask me to do it. I can match the colours well, I can tell you if the finished article is well-made or hanging straight. I know what it should look like - I just can't get it there myself.

So, when I heard about this jewellery workshop I was rather excited. At last, without needing to struggle, I could learn to make beautiful and useful things. I would take RT teen with me, as he is artistic on the outside as well as the inside and I also invited my cousin, who is 18 months older than me and obviously used up all the practical genes before I arrived.

It was only going to last an hour and a half, so even if it was bad or I was bad, then it wouldn't be too long before we were released out into the night.

It started, as so many things do, with me getting lost. After accosting an old man in the street, we found our way there and arrived 15 minutes behind everyone else. I was already playing catch up. There was another group using the same room, so while we made beautiful objects they appeared to be painting puppies. The room was awash with artistic intention.

RT teen and I made our way to the empty seats and looked at the bewildering array of tools and, erm, shiny-things-what-stick-stuff-together all laid out on little sponge mats on the tables. When I saw the tools I did panic a little as you can cut things with them and I have fingers, but then I had a little talk with myself and decided the lady running the group would most likely tell me how to use them without any harm coming to me.

We had to start by measuring our wrists with chain, as we were making a charm bracelet. Funny how often a piece of chain can fall off you before you catch it and measure it. Myself and RT teen sitting there, with identically swinging pieces of chain, both trying to catch them.

Then we had to choose beads and such to go on them. I instantly took against the charms box as they were all small and girly and looked like my inner five year old would like them. I went off to the bead box instead and chose all sorts of nice things. Actually, I confess. What I did was go to the bead box and feel panic setting in.

As I looked down at the compartments packed with beads I realised that there was too much choice and that I had no idea what I was doing. I loved the colours all shining up at me and their lovely shapes. I knew which ones I liked and which ones I didn't but was worried about choosing too many or the wrong ones or that I was taking too long.

RT teen had already chosen his and sat back down and the lady was getting ready to tell him what to do. I hurriedly chose my beads and went back to my seat, hoping it would be okay.

You can see how I was stressing myself out here, without any help from other people, but I didn't realise what I was doing.

I sat opposite the lady and she explained how you have to take the linking thingy and hold it with these special pliers, then pull it apart with other special pliers. And they have to be the *right* pliers. And, readers, at that point I realised I had no idea how to pull the linking thingy apart as I couldn't tell it *was* a linking thingy; it just looked like a solid circle to me. My eyesight was letting me down so badly that I couldn't see where the tiny gap was in the link, so didn't know where to hold it with the pliers and where to pull.

This nasty moment was compounded by the fact that once I had the thingy trapped in one set of pliers, I couldn't catch hold of it with the others because the nerves which started at the bead box had made their way into my hands and I was shaking. I had to physically take deep breaths to calm down so I could steady my hands enough to get the second set of pliers onto the linking thingy.

Once I had finally, painfully, achieved the impossible and prised the link apart, I realised I had to do this many times, obviously, as they were what held the charms on the bracelet.

What other people were having trouble with because it was unfamiliar was almost impossible for me as I couldn't even see what I was doing, and that was before understanding the procedure. I think this could be a handy metaphor for aspergers and life in general, don't you think? Other people find it tricky, learning how to do things the right way, but when you start from a point of not even being able to see the thing you're meant to be working on, then how can you achieve the same things as everyone else?

Shall I tell you how I achieved it, in this case at least? Readers, I'm slightly embarrassed to admit it, but I *felt* for the flipping gap in the link, then put it into the pliers, making sure not to lose my place. This worked remarkably well, my only hurdle then was getting hold of it with both sets of pliers at once as my left hand desperately wanted me to grip onto my right hand instead of the link. Such is the life of the aspie, one hand doing as you tell it while the other one rushes in to undo all your hard work.

Just when I thought I was getting the hang of it (hold on for another metaphor), I was told we had to thread an evil pin through the bigger beads then turn it in a special way to make a loop so it could be threaded onto yet more of the infernal thingys. The lady said that men usually found this bit easier as they were good with tools (mwwahahahahahah).

Cue indignant hoffing from both myself and RT teen as he is into equal rights (and pretty bad with tools anyway) and I am appallingly bad with tools but objected in principle to the idea that this meant I would also be bad at bending an evil pin into a loop shape.

It turns out that this, at least, I could do. My loops were great and I could see the beggars. I could easily follow the instructions on how they should be turned because they were logical and made sense. Also, it brought back memories of my happy days in school sewing classes when I would amuse myself by bending needles and pins into artistic shapes before using them to pull threads through my thumb.

By this time, I was feeling like I could be getting the hang of things with the hideous charm bracelet, which left me enough attention to eavesdrop on everyone else. It was then I realised how out of step I was with the rest of the room - or at least, I felt like I was.

The conversations going on around me had that odd, otherworldly quality where you sit there, just being yourself and feeling okay, then other people come along and talk about their lives and you suddenly feel like a pimple on the behind of a massive alien.

They were talking about shopping and TV and concerts and drinking and all kinds of things that were ordinary events in their lives. I was listening to the words and knew it was all fine, they were real people and I was real people too, but still feeling as if I would be revealed, at any moment, as someone who was in the wrong place.

How does this happen? You're in a room full of friendly, cheerful people, most of whom would be considered your peers by anyone looking in from the outside, when you yourself feel as if they might turn on you and rip you apart if you put a foot wrong? How strange it is that we do this to ourselves, make such a detour with the mind so that a friendly situation becomes threatening and makes us feel we need to escape.

Oh dear, the more I write about it on here, the more I see why I was so stressed! At the time I was concentrating so hard on not looking like Mr Magoo does jewellery, that I kind of lost sight of the fact I was having a whole new experience, filled with new people in a new place at the end of a very busy day. This is where you could do with a narrator who could step in and say:

Amanda was feeling very tired by the end of the day and shouldn't have been surprised she found the situation so difficult. Instead, she blamed herself for being half-blind and an introvert and hoped she could come back the next week without finding the doors locked against her.

I think I'll do without the narrator, on reflection. I narrate enough of my own life and find that distracting at times so it would be even worse if I had a disembodied voice explaining things when I'm trying to concentrate on just getting through the day.

When we returned, alive, from the jewellery workshop, we showed IT teen our charm bracelets. RT teen's looked lovely, a symmetrical delight in pinks, purples and silver charms. Mine looked like I'd been running from something as I made it, which wasn't too far from the truth.

I told IT teen I didn't want any proper food for supper, I would just have cereal as I felt sick. He had a mini-rant, telling me I wasn't sick, I had just spent an hour and a half with strangers and that was all that was wrong with me, He said I shouldn't always come away feeling ill, just because I've had to be sociable. He made me have supper and I felt almost human again.

I did feel properly sick, readers, I would swear it wasn't phantasmagorical. But then, why should it be? I was having a real physical reaction to something that had felt like real physical danger. At the very least, the stress was real.

So, today, I'm not really surprised that I've been moaning and unable to think straight. By the end of yesterday, I was already tired and then had my adrenaline firing at the workshop. Today I needed to recharge and feel steady again and I've only reached that point now, after writing about it.

It takes so much effort sometimes, to just live your life and behave in the right way. It's no wonder that we can't understand why we feel or act the way we do, when it's taken everything we have just to play our role in life itself. Sometimes, we don't know things are too much until they are and then it's usually too late as we're in the middle of events, with no easy way out.

Last night was a friendly little workshop, aimed at helping me make jewellery. Thanks to my annoying tendency to make life as dramatic as possible, it turned into a struggle for survival and a series of high emotions all centered around a little bracelet with beads and charms hanging off it at odd angles.

Really, though, last night was a reminder of how aspergers can rear its head at the most unexpected moments, when you think you have everything pegged out just right and know what goes where. You have to learn to shrug it off and not worry too much. It's no good blaming yourself for taking things too seriously or for not seeing them coming: the truth of it will always be that life is as it will be and we are always going to be ourselves in the middle of it.

There are always going to be adventures where we don't expect them and where other people could never see them. That's part of the excitement of being an aspie, you never know quite what to expect.

Seriously, though, the next time I mention any kind of workshop, can someone just distract me into the book store instead? That's so much more *me*...

THE PART-TIME DISABILITY

Before I start receiving hate mail, this is not my view! Obviously, aspergers can't be switched on and off, or even turn itself on and off. Sometimes it *seems* to, especially when stress levels rise, but that's not what I mean by this phrase.

I'm talking about when people close to you, whether family, friends, best beloveds or co-workers, who know about your aspergers, give you credence for it one day and expect you to behave normally the next. Those occasions when you're as aspie as you were the day before, but for whatever reason, they expect you not to behave like you are, because it's not convenient.

This is one of the major downsides of having a hidden disability, which often occurs in people who can function at a high level a lot of the time. You're already looking okay because you can manage all kinds of everyday tasks. Those of who us who are adults have had to incorporate our daily lives into our aspie-ness, making one support the other as much as possible.

We can often come across well, listening to people, talking to them and doing what is needed. When we're having a high-aspie day, the people close to us can tell and, depending on the relationship, make allowances, try to help, ignore it or carry on as usual.

It starts to go wrong when the person with you decides they need the 'other' you, the one who can manage things and do stuff and be an all-round Mr or Ms Normal. This other you doesn't really exist, it's just the front you put on for most of your life. It helps you get through and makes things seem better. It drops on the bad days and cracks under pressure even on the good ones.

So a scenario may be when the other person needs you to do something for them. Let's say they're the ones needing support, or they are having a bad day and don't have time to mollycoddle you. Or it just isn't important in the grand scheme of things that you're an aspie as x, y and z need to get done.

It's at times like this when someone who has known for years that you have aspergers, can turn round and expect you to do everything as if you are a normally wired, fully-functioning, non-eccentric and definitely non-aspie human bean. On that day they need you to be like everyone else and you can almost guarantee that'll be a day when you're feeling like an unsoaked bean, rather than a baked one with tomato sauce.

Of course, we don't help ourselves, do we? Rather than being permanently awkward and aspie, we *do* have good days when we can do loads of stuff. Often, it should be said, the stuff we do on these good days is not what other people would see as important, but we still manage it. So why can't we step up and be like that when the other person needs us? In their mind, they've stepped up for us many times, can't we return the favour?

It doesn't come across like that, though. Just because we manage well a lot of the time, or seem to, doesn't mean *this time*, when you need help with x, y and z, we'll be able to provide it. Worse, after years of conditioning that things must be done a certain way and we have to be a certain kind of person, we'll go ahead and try to do what is asked of us, regardless of how we feel. It's the knee-jerk reaction of the adult aspie who has struggled to fit in their whole lives.

And worse than this, suppose you're particularly good at something and that's one area where people can turn to you for help? Great, a confidence booster and a way to repay them for putting up with your Fringe obsession or your latest humdinger of a conversation-stopper. What if your aspie-meter rises at the time they need help with this area and you suddenly find you can't do it? Lead balloon, anyone?

In my case, I've always enjoyed filling in forms - sad but true. Then I had to fill in some forms this summer and I don't know whether it's the extra stress I've had this year, or a decrease in sleep and caffeine or what, but suddenly the forms made much less sense than before. I had to fill them in, they were properly official and other people were relying on me.

I looked and studied them, I worked through them. I wrote my answers separately so I wouldn't get them wrong. I looked up online guides and peered at the help pages. I managed to struggle through most of the form but was still worried it was wrong or that I'd missed something. Even then, there were a couple of questions I just couldn't do.

I must admit to getting upset over them. It was all down to me, I was the only one who could fill them in. I had all the information I thought they needed, I just couldn't make it fit the form. In desperation, I went and had a soak in the bath.

After a long bath and time to calm down, I decided to put aside the panic and look again, calmly and methodically, at the form. There, at the top of it, now sticking out for all to see, was a question I had missed which made sense of the ones I couldn't work out. The answer had been there all along, I just wasn't able to see it.

I completed the form and sent it off and all was well - that time. It shook me, though. This was a task I would have breezed through a year or so ago, yet this time I could barely manage the normal questions. It was like I had grit in the gears and they couldn't move smoothly, so each stage I completed was a separate thing from the rest of the form and I couldn't keep my concentration going long enough to succeed all in one go.

It's at times like this you worry that aspergers matures like old cheese and that by the time I hit fifty, I'll be running naked through Tesco, having finally dumped all my inhibitions along with my common sense.

And amongst all this drama and the belief that I'm now on a downhill slope towards complete eccentricity, is the little voice of people who still want that form, did you do the form? it doesn't usually take this long...

How can you tell people your brain decided forms were no-go? When people want something from you and you say you're having a bad day, there is a blank reaction, because they expected you to manage the thing they want done. To them, it sounds like you're being wishy-washy. After all, it's not as if they can do it any better - you always do it!

So, I got the form done and didn't go into the trouble I'd had with it. I just said it was quite difficult and I'd had a struggle to finish it. I didn't mention lying in the bath, wondering who could help me or if it would ever get done.

I'm cutting myself a break, though. As I've said, it's been a heck of a year, so it's not surprising that, alongside normal stresses, there might be a deeper, underlying stress, slumbering just under the surface, waiting for extra responsibilities to prod it awake. I'm going to write off the form fiasco as a fluke, something brought on by lots of other things. I'll try not to carry it with me when I need to do another.

As for people expecting the part-time aspie, I'm also cutting myself a break there. If I can come out on here, on Facebook and to the world at large, I can certainly turn round to the person expecting Ms Normal and remind them that I'm not her! If they want Ms Normal, they need to look elsewhere. Here is only Ms Cheese, maturing into goodness knows what.

THERE'S NOTHING WRONG WITH YOU!

How often have we heard that? Or, as the parent of a child with aspergers, heard that there's nothing wrong with our child that some discipline wouldn't sort out.

Aspergers doesn't leave physical signs that people can tick off on their disability checklist. If you know what to look for, you may be able to spot a fellow aspie at ten paces - there is such a thing as aspie-dar. Otherwise, you're left wondering if a person is on the autistic spectrum or just out to drive you crazy. (It should be noted, some people *are* just out to drive you crazy and I'm still undecided if there are more of them than there are aspies in the world).

Girls with aspergers possibly suffer less from being threatened with discipline, as aspergers in girls is often harder to diagnose. In my experience, girls tend to suffer on the inside in a way that doesn't always show itself on the outside; or at least, they don't display their suffering in a way that makes people think there may be something more going on.

Again, in my experience, boys are more extrovert in their aspieness. I don't mean they are more likely to be extroverts, but their behaviour is more noticeable. They act out, are more obviously 'naughty' and so on. They are the ones who get to meet the headmistress, while aspie girls sit in mute isolation, not getting into trouble as much but not coping any better either.

This is all generalisation, though, aimed at explaining the main issues. Everyone is different and every aspie is different. I have known girls on the spectrum who burst into a room, their aura a blaze of colour as they burn across the room, then collapse in floods of tears when the reaction wasn't as expected or they couldn't cope. I've known boys who sit, like monoliths, impassive, unmoved, no visible reactions to things they find hilarious and who only emerge very gradually from their shells, once you know them much better.

Both of these examples can be firmly on the spectrum, both can be properly aspie, but will be viewed as loud and inappropriate, or too quiet and unsociable. Their school reports may differ in the advice for their behaviour, but will probably come together as teachers say they can achieve more if they would just **try harder**, which makes the child look lazy or inattentive.

There's nothing wrong with them, you see. They are only misbehaving, or not behaving in the right way. If they would only do as they are told, they'd be fine.

I have to add that my comments can be applied to the diagnosed aspie, too. For anyone considering a diagnosis, either for themselves or their child, be aware it is not a golden ticket to better understanding and treatment. It's not the label or the diagnosis which brings you these things, it's the people you meet along the way. A teacher or employer who is open-minded about you or your child is likely to treat them just as well and with as much understanding, with or without a diagnosis.

It can be so frustrating as a parent of an aspie child, when you are trying to make people see how they need to be treated. When my son started school, I explained until their eyes glazed over how he shouldn't be unsupervised, he needed clear guidance. I was as straightforward as possible.

This didn't prevent the school disregarding nearly everything I said. They once went on a short trip to the local church. It was five minutes away, on foot. They made the children walk two-by-two. I had already told them they should hold my son's hand if they were ever out of school as he loved to run off. Instead, they let him hold another boy's hand and explained to him he mustn't let go.

Halfway to school, while walking along a street with cars parked on both sides, my son saw something on the opposite side of the road and took off after it. He remembered he mustn't let go of the other boy and, gripping him firmly, took the boy with him into the middle of the road, from between parked cars. They were very lucky, there was nothing coming.

At the end of the day, as usual, I was taken to one side and told how naughty he had been and what had happened. I was appalled at what might have been, as much for the innocent boy he took with him as for my son himself. I admitted how I felt but told them again that I had said, more than once, he shouldn't be out of school without a teacher holding his hand. The teacher talking to me looked irritated, like I was trying to get him out of trouble, and told me they had explained to him fully what he needed to do.

What can you say that you haven't said already? I had explained the reasons behind keeping a good hold of him outside school. I had told them how he took off whenever he could and had no understanding of the consequences and no sense of danger. I had been as clear as I could with people who should have listened. After that, you leave your child in their care and hope for the best.

It was never resolved with that school and we changed schools later. New teachers and different treatment from staff meant my son could enjoy his school days again and be safe.

I've covered in another post (http://aspie-girl.blogspot.co.uk/2012/10/the-myth-of-under-achiever.html) what it was like for me going through school and work as an undiagnosed aspie. There was nothing visibly wrong with me and I could behave, more or less, like a normal person. I could hold conversations, learn new things, perform when necessary...until I couldn't.

You see, as an aspie, you can do lots of things, quite a lot of the time. To the untrained eye, there is nothing wrong with you. People differ, but a lot of aspies can manage things most of the time, often because they have learned coping strategies or learned to avoid situations they can't cope with. So, at first glance, there is nothing the matter. Then you get the days when things go wrong, or unexpected events shake the aspie's world, or they just wake up and it's a no-go day. Then you're stuck with being unreliable and needing to get across to people why you can't do today what you have done all week.

Why not? would be the question people might ask, if you were completely honest and said, 'I just can't today'. If you haven't been diagnosed or haven't come out as an aspie, then what do you say? It's no good saying you're having a bad day, or feeling down. Then you really sound like you're not pulling your weight. You make something up, that's what you do. You give an acceptable reason why you can't come in today.

I was doing a temporary job, full-time for a few months. It was public-facing, occasionally stressful, working with lots of people. It required organisation and attention to detail. It was all day, for five days a week and I didn't even leave at lunchtime.

By the second month, I felt like the walls were closing in on me. I would go to the bathroom just to have a break and sit in the toilet cubicle, door locked, head in my hands, bent double. I can't tell you how many times I've hidden in toilets in my life! The bliss of a locked door.

I had to take time off and I had no good reason. I also didn't understand what was wrong with me. I'd been pleased to get the job, I really needed the money. I wasn't ill, I wasn't properly stressed, nothing in particular had happened. I just knew I couldn't go in. It was like a force field: every time I thought of work, I bounced right off it.

I told them I had a bug and would be off for the rest of the week. I had three days, then the weekend. So, five days before I had to face work again. I spent the first day in town with my mother, as she did her errands. I stood outside shops, waiting for her, because I couldn't stand to be inside, where there were lots of people and enclosed spaces. I went to town with her because I couldn't stand to be at home either.

I remember standing outside one shop, facing across the road. I was looking at a theatre, the Carnegie, to anyone who is local to me. I used to go in the theatre's cafe when my Grandma looked after me, before I started school. I remembered sitting in there, the smoky atmosphere of cigarettes, the gossip of my Grandma and her friends. I sat with three ladies of a certain age, me a small child, content to spend my days with them. The background noise of their gossip and the world around us all was a safe place for me because I was looked after and not expected to participate. It was a peaceful time.

Now, all those years later, I stood and stared at the Carnegie. I touched that place in the past, where I was small and safe. The little me, with the scuffed knees and red shoes; she was satisfied and content. The bigger me needed some of that light, that contentment and safety. Enclosed in my memory, I heard the voices of my Grandma and her friends, their laughter. I felt my hand in hers, my fingers warm under the edge of her coat sleeve.

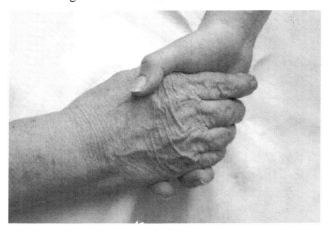

I knew, then, that I wasn't the person I had expected to be. It was at that moment, faced with the happy child I had been, that I saw I wasn't happy now. I realised that, for whatever reason, my life didn't fit me. The life then had fitted me. I had felt safe and now I didn't.

Reader, if I hadn't been so numb and weak emotionally, I would have cried as I stood there. Not tears of self-pity, or sadness at not being safe in my Grandma's hands anymore, but tears of confusion because I didn't know what was wrong with me. I just knew that there was *something* wrong.

And there, that was the moment when I started this journey. That was where I began to explore *why* I was different. Not just eccentric, or odd, or from a family where that could pass as normal. Why I was unfit for purpose in the modern world, what it was about me that made me fear the very places I needed to be.

I've made it here, to you. I know more about myself now than I ever expected to know. I thought, by now, I would know everything. I'm often amazed how much there is still to learn. I needed to suffer then to understand myself now.

I have to tell you, I still sometimes hide in toilets. I still sometimes need to remember the feel of my Grandma's coat sleeve covering my fingers. I'm never going to be so strong that I don't need to look back at a time when I was small and weak and felt absolutely safe.

The difference now is, I know what is wrong with me. And it's not wrong. I just happen to have aspergers, that's all.

SELF-ESTEEM

This is a biiiig subject and, like communication, slips almost unseen through the whole of aspie life. It's surprising and disheartening to see how many people with Aspergers labour under low self-esteem. It just makes me so angry! It's one of those things I understand and can explain, but really hate about Aspergers.

Part of my main motivation behind doing the blog was to make people realise they are not alone, that they have these feelings and problems for a reason and not because they are a failure, or are silly, or unfeeling or too sensitive or any of the names we give ourselves when we feel we're to blame.

I want people to see that self-esteem is just another stick to beat ourselves with and exists because we coped with the world, but were a little dented from the encounter.

I don't think aspies can totally avoid low self-esteem. The world is very big and there are so many people in it that, sooner or later, we will come up against someone or something that hurts us. The trouble with aspies is, hurt stays in place for much longer and is referred back to at leisure: this is the main reason self-esteem is such an issue.

If you hold on to past hurts, then they will have an effect on your present and it will never be a good one. Getting beyond them and breaking free is possible, with time and patience, it just needs more time and more patience than for a non-aspie.

Don't despair, though, it isn't all bleak. While writing the blog and realising the role self-esteem played in my own life, I also came to another major epiphany: we must forgive ourselves for being affected in this way. It's no good being determined to react differently the next time or to put it all behind you; you must also be loving towards yourself and say, 'It's okay, I know I was upset, I know that hurt me, but it's just the way I am.'

To move on, you need to have the ability to take yourself with you and be happy with the company. Self-esteem issues are never going to vanish entirely, but you can learn to cope with them and rise above the trap of pushing yourself back down because of them.

SELF-ESTEEM! CAN YOU HEAR ME SHOUTING YET?

I cannot emphasise this enough: self-esteem is fundamental to aspergers in adults. Yes, it's very important to aspie children too - who isn't in need of some self-esteem, aspie or not? But for the aspie adult, it underpins every single negative feeling and thought process they have ever had. I'm not exaggerating.

You can be a fruity-loop aspie, like me, who loves to shoot off and do creative things without a backward glance and only half an eye on the consequences. You can be a super-introvert and only talk to those you trust the most, always conscious of yourself and your surroundings. You can be living in happy oblivion, just thinking you're a bit odd, like Great Uncle Horace, and it never did him any harm. You can be any version of aspie you like and self-esteem is with you every step of the way, like a small dog after your biscuits.

I mention my own version of aspie-ness first as, to the un-trained eye, I am probably the least visibly affected by self-esteem issues. I go about my business, my mood swings are often on the up as I have filtered out any negatives from the situation at hand. As I've said before, in my life I have normal responsibilities which I fulfill to the best of my abilities. I don't look like I have self-esteem issues. If you ask me about something I'm doing, I'll usually tell you the positives and leave out any downsides, so you come away thinking I don't have any big issues.

In the comfort of my own mind, I also try to ignore the negatives and carry on as if life is a bed of pansies (last longer than roses and no thorns). I'm confident in my abilities and can do what needs to be done.

Yes. Hmm. So, has it ever occurred to you why some people are relentlessly positive? I am not, by the way. People close to me hear the other side of it, the downside, the worries. So, that means other people, who show their sunny-side first, they have their worries and anxieties too. But does the world see them? No.

Positivity is a brilliant, life-giving force. It can inspire people, it can carry you along in the midst of dreadfulness, it can be the fuel you need to get by, let alone succeed. This is the secret known to the relentlessly positive. You'll often find, if you dig deep, that the more positive, upbeat, annoyingly optimistic people you know have a depth of sadness within them. They will have experienced pain and loss. They probably won't talk about it often. They still feel it, though. The reason for the upbeat part is that they know life is too short, and sometimes too hard, to let the dark cloud get you. Keep moving, keep jogging, dance if you have to, but don't stand still or it might catch up.

What does this have to do with self-esteem, you may be wondering. Everything, unfortunately. For, while a person may elect to be upbeat after hardship, as a way of coping with life, it is their self-esteem which prevents them from coming to you, their friend, and admitting how bad they feel today. If they had self-confidence, you would know how they felt, they would tell you things more often. And then you could help them.

It's a sad kind of closed-off world where the more jolly types, always with a smile, are the ones least likely to burden others with their problems. You don't want to know about them! Much better that they know about *you*, so they can help you and spread some more positive energy about.

The reason for such spreading is that they have received rather less kindness and good energy themselves than they needed. They have been left adrift, in some way, perhaps by circumstance, more likely by other people. To be fair, if you are already the sort of person who can present a public front - and so many aspie women are - then you have not given others the chance to know you need support. But there is always a starting point for this front, for the pretence and the belief others won't be there for them.

As a child, it can start very early. Most children soak things up and learn quickly how other people are. They'll learn that Grandpa is grumpy and Grandma gives them cake. They'll know not to bother cousin Henry's chickens or he goes purple in the face. They know that Auntie Lucy doesn't like her ornaments touched, but will let you watch cartoons when you visit.

The aspie child is no different. They also learn these lessons about people, but they are already processing lessons about everything - how you cross the road, how to tie your shoes, why you don't keep your coat on indoors, how not to slam the car door, where to sit when you visit people, when to speak and when to be quiet.

Imagine growing up with so many on-going lessons in your head. Each new one is added to the list and recited, consciously or not. A bit like an old film reel, it spins past, each image adding to the whole, each sound supposed to connect to the right scene. Then, on top of this, you must remember how to behave with people too? It can be a little too much.

So, sometimes, because of the overload, you forget about not touching Auntie Lucy's ornament. It doesn't break but she's not very happy. She's kind and explains to you how sad she would be if you had broken it and that's why she doesn't let you touch them. She promises, when you're older, you can hold them.

You like Auntie Lucy, you are horrified that you've upset her. You vow never to touch the ornaments again, and because you remember her being upset, you remember not to touch them - that part is fine. But you remember it was you, you forgetful, silly thing, who upset her in the first place. The rest of the visit is spent under a cloud. You know she'll let you touch them when you're older; this translates as when you're good enough to touch them, when you can be trusted. That turns backwards and comes to mean now, at this moment, you can't be trusted and you're not good enough.

Yes, it may sound convoluted, but the mind of the aspie is constantly turning, doubling back, re-processing everything in order to make it all understandable. Even if you do understand it, you're so used to getting it wrong, you repeat the process anyway, to make sure you have it right this time.

Even a simple thing, like a harsh word, sticks to an aspie like a burr on a dog's coat. You look at cousin Henry's chickens and he says, 'No!', giving you a look. You were never going to touch them but you feel the sting of his tone and his expression. It's a small thing, but away it goes, on the never-ending film reel, waiting to pass by a few times, so you can spot it amongst the rest.

You see, due to the over-sensitive nature of most aspies, when they are properly plugged in and listening, or when an event makes them remember something (like upsetting Auntie Lucy), they hold onto it like nobody's business. And you can't run that film reel in an eternal loop past your consciousness, not without a gargantuan memory and no ability to focus on the outside world. So, as time passes, earlier events are shelved away and new ones take their place. Strong, brightly-coloured memories, stay on the reel and pass by occasionally.

What remains are the *feelings* engendered by certain situations and the lessons those feelings taught you about yourself. You add the feelings to the image you have of you, the person, the personality. You become the clumsy one (this is possibly true) and the knowledge you are clumsy, or perceived as clumsy, becomes bundled up in the sad feelings from the past.

Without ever realising it, you have inserted a little, muddy, nasty brick in the wall of your life and there it stays, only visible when you go close up but still a part of the whole you.

So, by the time you're an adult, your endless learning process has already incorporated many negative lessons about your personality. You are always ready to learn more, too. As an adult aspie, you still haven't got a grip on the world and how it works. If someone says 'this is so' then it is, because someone else said it, and other people know things you don't.

I suppose it's true to say that self-esteem, for the aspie, is tied up with **self-trust**: you learn not to trust yourself, after all the times you made mistakes, so other people, by definition, are more trust-worthy. Follow this on and it means that whatever they say about you must be true. If someone else gives you conflicting information, confusion ensues and you tend to believe whoever you're with at the time, being left with the negative sense of still not knowing who you are.

I don't have the answers to this problem, I'm afraid. I do have some answers for people living with their aspies, and who feel frustration at trying to build the self-confidence of their loved one. It can seem like, no matter what you say or do, your aspie will throw it back in your face, by word or thought or deed. It doesn't matter how much you love them or what proof you have they are a good, kind, intelligent, creative person: your aspie will deny it, even if that denial is only happening within their own mind.

You can't undo years of bad education here. Your aspie has learned relentlessly and is still learning. Yes, your opinions and words will be filed away on the current film reel, and they'll probably appreciate you making the effort. Unfortunately, they may also resent you for bringing up their personality again and harping on about how good, kind etc they are when they don't want to hear it!

Sometimes, at a later stage in life, aspies have done such a good job in learning who they are via other people, they reach overload and can only process new information which seems relevant. If they have bad self-esteem, then good feedback may not appear relevant, as they know good things don't really apply to them. This is why you will sometimes get the tetchy response when you're being nice to them.

What can you do? The short answer: not much except be there. But the long answer, that's a good one...

The long answer is great. Give it time, hang in there, be subtle in your building-up of your beloved's self-esteem. Barely let them know you're doing it. If you have definite proof of their brilliance (ie the computer is working again because of them), **include the proof in your words**. They may still brush it off but proof is gold to an aspie and often gets filed away when your words don't.

If other people have said good things about them, mention it at the same time as you backing up the comments. Hearing that more than one person thinks they're an okay person is often more persuasive. BUT, do not stand there, with that other person, and tell the aspie together. That means an instant irritation and overload - two people talking at once is a terrible thing! You'll lose any benefit from the negative reaction to being overwhelmed.

I'll leave it there for now. You can see by the length of this post that self-esteem is a major factor in aspie life and aspergers behaviour. I will re-visit it later and cover the areas I've had to leave out today.

I'll finish with one thought: aspies do not see themselves as being the same as other people, which means good words and opinions may only apply to others and not to them. If you say something good to them, don't make it a blanket statement of 'you are good because...' Instead, always say, '**I think** you are good because...'

Making it your own, specific opinion helps a little when it comes to them believing you. It's a subtle difference, but it can work when other words fail.

ASPIE: CHILD VS ADULT

I've been thinking a lot about my childhood self and how things have changed since then - how I have changed. It made me wonder how I could describe the difference between having aspergers as a child and what it's like to be an aspie adult.

I think I can sum it up in one word - responsibility.

As a child, however your aspie nature presents itself, you have little or no **responsibilities.** I would say that the big one for most aspie children is the need to go to school. The strain of school, the damage it can do and the way that stress can exaggerate the behaviours of aspergers, is often the reason why a fair number of parents decide to home educate their autistic spectrum children. (I'll go into home education more in a later post, as it is a very good way to look at aspergers and the effects of normal school).

So, to an aspie child, school is enormously important. It comprises a large part of their daily lives, and even if they enjoy it, school is something which has to be done, so it becomes a big responsibility.

As an adult aspie, it can be a whole nightmare of responsibility, depending on the lifestyle you follow.

As I've said before, I have a lot of different responsibilities, but so do other aspie adults. I'm talking about things that, if avoided, can make your life fall apart.

Keeping up the bills, running a car, raising children, looking after other people, holding down a job. Every aspie adult could give you a slightly different list of responsibilities, but if they have a mainstream lifestyle, they are likely to be looking after others, or being responsible for them in some way.

So, as an adult, responsibility is really foremost in the mind. It is the central hub around which your whole life revolves. You can never really forget it, even if things are going well. If you're lucky and have a job you can cope with or you enjoy, the responsibility element of work fades away a little. If you find being a parent a wonderful, life-fulfilling role, the responsibility of that can shrink compared to the benefits.

It never goes away, though. It's always there and you need to keep one eye on it at all times.

Unlike when you were a child, there is no one to pick up the pieces. Even if you have a partner to help you as an adult, or your parents still pitch in, you are still in the middle of life and expected to be a grown person who does things and can cope with things. You may have a moan or a fret and your nearest and dearest probably know more of your stresses than others, but they do still expect you to get up the next day and do it all again.

As a child you can have a meltdown and the worst that can happen is your parents will have a few more grey hairs or be judged, again, by the neighbours. As an adult, if you go for the full melt-down, you're likely to be carted off by the police or ambulance crew. Inside, the same emotions which brought you to tears as a child, they still mill about, washing over you, trying to take over and make you give in to the all-out pandemonium of losing control.

Mostly, as adults, we don't lose control in this way. We can hold it together long enough to at least make it home and hide in the bathroom. Sometimes you need to control this feeling in stages, so you do what you can where you can, perhaps by going into the car and sitting quietly or finding a less busy corner of the department store and pretending to look at things while you take some deep breaths.

The difference as an adult is not just that you know it will cause so much embarrassment and bother to be seen, on the floor, gnashing the carpet and kicking your legs; you are also aware that you can control it a little and don't need to behave this way to cope. You know if you can just make it to point A, then point B is over there, point C is outside in the car park, point D will be within sight at the traffic lights and point E is the blessed sound of you opening the house door. (This is a coping mechanism I'll cover in another post as it works so well for me, most of the time).

So, as an adult, we can persuade ourselves to calm down a little, or, more likely, to hang on for now, you can lose it later when you're alone. The difference here is that by doing this, you *don't* lose it later. You get past point E, the door closes and life is still there but the meltdown feeling isn't. At best, you're back to where you started - feeling sad or stressed and with your emotions under control but not helping you at all.

One good thing about having a meltdown is that even when you factor in the exhaustion which follows, you got those feelings all stirred up and thrown out of your system at once. The adult response means you don't usually get arrested, but you do have to carry on with the same feelings. It's a bit like the difference between a pan boiling over. The meltdown gets rid of the problem (the steam) all at once but isn't beneficial afterwards; the calmer adult is like lifting the lid to let out just enough steam so you save the peas and they carry on cooking. Better for the peas (the responsibilities), but much less good for getting rid of all that steam you built up.

The pan of peas looks like a bad example at first glance. Isn't it better to use that steam to cook the peas more quickly? Don't we want it to stay in there, not be all over he cooker with little blackened husks cooked to the bottom of the pan? Yes and no. The answer to that lies in how you view responsibilities.

When it comes to living life in a successful way, you need to cope with everything as well as you can. When you're living with aspergers, the responsibilities are always secondary to you, and the way you cope with things. The peas in the pan are important, but to an aspie the steam is always there, cooking or not and must be released or else we go very mad indeed.

This is partly a problem of perspective as well as mental and emotional health. From the outside, other people will see that responsibilities come first and the aspie needs to adapt and get on with it. From the inside, the aspie knows all responsibilities equal stress, so even the small ones, that they can cope with, become bigger than they are and intuitively linked to the bigger ones anyway.

The key, as an adult, without someone always there to pick up the pieces, give you support and tuck you in at night, is to recognise

what needs doing when. This is the same approach as points A-E above. Use it for responsibilities too. A simple example would be, do not avoid paying your rent! If you run out of money, do not pay the Sky bill first. Know which needs the most attention from you.

If you're having a bad few days and want to ignore everything, ask for help. Other people can do a lot of things for you and sometimes you need them. Do not pretend it will wait or go away because sometimes it won't.

If you have no one to ask, be kind to yourself. Some things can't wait, but you need to be able to do them without making any big mistakes. If you have a few important things which need your attention, think a little about them and decide which is the most urgent. Stop, go away, come back. Do the most urgent part of the most urgent thing. Stop, go away, come back. When you're ready, repeat the process.

Responsibilities are never going to go away and, really and truly, if you had no stresses at all in life, you'd be SO bored. Honestly, I'm telling the truth here, you know I wouldn't lie to you! I know that things can be hard and stressful and you often wish you were like a child again, with someone else doing all the nasty stuff for you. I can't take away all the stress and I can't do the nasty stuff for you. But if you break it up into pieces, it will get done and by trying different ways of coping, you'll learn new tricks and new methods of doing it better the next time.

So, yes, the main difference between being a child with aspergers or an adult is the simple matter of responsibilities, coupled with the very complicated matter of still being an aspie once you're all grown up. That's the secret, folks. We may walk and talk and can cook you dinner, but on the inside we're still the awkward kid who laughed when nothing was funny in the middle of the school play.

Be patient and remember to ask us how we're getting on. And maybe when the rent is due.

THE ICE COLD MELTDOWN

We all know about the aspie meltdown, that complete lack of control, loosening of inhibitions, the inability to hold back all the feelings that must get out and *now*. Yes, the meltdown is familiar territory. But what about the aspie at the other end of the scale? What happens when you have had enough of something, just enough, no more will be taken, nothing more will be said, but you follow a different route from the traditional meltdown? What happens then?

It's what you might call the emergence of the **ice cold meltdown**. Let me explain.

If something is bothering me, then it's bothering me. There are no shortcuts to peace of mind, I can't 'just ignore it', I can't 'get over it' and I sure as heck don't feel like talking about it. Not after the other times I've talked about it and been told I'm over-reacting, or everyone goes through this or, instead, had to hear about how I've always been this way and it's about time I learned to deal with things.

Faced with an on-going problem - and I mean a big one - those of us who internalise and tend to feel trapped in situations, do have the choices. As said, we can wait until it becomes explosive and meltdown, we can rumble along, becoming more mired down in it all until we crack in some other way - or we can do something about it.

Now, when I say do something about it, don't get me wrong. I don't mean that we resolve it in some sane way that other people would see as a resolution. I don't suggest we face it head on and calmly negotiate ourselves through this rocky patch. No, I'm talking about direct action.

Whether it's a full-blown, short-acting plan, such as a tremendous exit from work, or a longer, plotted course that takes in all the variables and presents us with an alternative, I know there are other aspies like me out there, who plot their way out of trouble.

For those of you without this streak of reckless self-endangerment, let me explain. If I'm in a part of my life where every step feels like ten, I look around for solutions. This is rational, yes? But I'll usually be in overdrive when I'm looking for those solutions, so the ideas I come up with sound great to me, but are usually on shaky ground. I guess we're talking about justifying things to your-self, so that you have a good excuse to stop putting up with an up-setting situation.

It's rather like the lifestyle version of a Get Rich Quick scheme. It all sounds great on paper, there doesn't seem to be a way that it could fail and, like the people who sign up for these (I've done it, I know how it feels), you don't want to see any pitfalls because that would mean going on as you are and having to look for another way out.

So, the aspie is in the role of the salesman of the scheme, de-termined to sell its benefits and push aside any possible flaws. As the salesman *and* the buyer, we aspies are adept at seeing things as we want them to be seen. We tell ourselves we're being sensible with this grand solution to our problems. Yes, there might be diffi-culties, but they'll be so small, it won't matter. This will work; we'll get out of trouble and we won't be hurting any more.

Then, like the scheme, money is handed over (sometimes liter-ally, sometimes we're handing over a part of our lives, like a rela-tionship, or a job) and we wait for the magic to happen. Does it? Well, at first it *feels* like it does, as the anticipation of change brings the illusion of change itself. Then reality sets in and we see we've swapped one problem for another. Again.

It wouldn't be so bad if these plans were small scale. I don't know about other aspies, but I don't generally do small scale plans. If I have a small idea, it quickly grows to a humungosaur idea and tramps around, roaring that it can take over the world. It never does, but, as usual, it feels like it's going to, this time.

The ice cold meltdown shows itself as the plotting and planning part of this new solution. I don't just fling myself in and plan later. Even though I rush into things, I do a lot of planning first and as I'm rushing along. I look at it all as if it's a beautiful problem to be solved and, again like magic, the solutions line themselves up. Never the problems, only the solutions.

Like a meltdown, the ice cold meltdown is a response to trouble but lasts longer and is calculated.

Shall I tell you how I think this approach started? It's an exciting story, terrifying really, and I feel wary of sharing it. But as I've already shared so much here, why not go for one of the big ones? I'm sure some of you have done, or attempted, worse...

As children, we're powerless. I was the same, a small, bespectacled girl with fluffy hair, unfashionable glasses and scuffed knees. I didn't know how to get on with other children very well, they always seemed to be talking about things I didn't understand. Looking back, this was partly the school I went to, as when I changed school and the teachers made an effort to integrate me, I made friends right away.

At my infant school, I was in the final year, waiting out my time before I could leave the dreadful place behind. I had been bullied all the way through the year. I'd told my parents and my teachers. No one took it seriously, all children name call, you just have to ignore it. A very lonely place for a little girl with no friends.

Every day I would go in and get through it as well as I could. My teacher liked me, one of the dinner ladies was a kind neighbour of my aunty. And that was it, frankly, the two people at school who would be pleased to see me. There may have been children who were potential friends, but I was unable to see them or work it out, so I was alone.

At the age of seven, I knew I couldn't bear it anymore. I could not keep going into that school, day after day, listening to the words they called after me, seeing their faces turn ugly as they looked my way. The closest I ever got to playtime was joining in group games and still I couldn't get it right and would be left standing as the others ran away.

I used to have daydreams about someone, some hero, crashing in through the school walls and taking me away from it all. The hero changed, the story changed but always I was rescued and taken away.

A few days before it happened, I decided if no one would help me or rescue me, I would do it myself. I could see no other way. As a seven year old, I had tried all other options. Now, it was down to me.

I thought hard and saw, clearly as anything, that if the school wasn't there, then I wouldn't have to go. Simple. From here it was a small jump to deciding to burn down the school. Yes, your read it right - your friendly blogger was a seven year old, wannabe arsonist. Actually, I wasn't. I was a seven year old victim, desperately looking for a way to make it STOP.

My parents both smoked and it was a simple matter to steal some matches. I put them in my bedroom cabinet and waited a couple of days, so that when the school was a steaming pile of junk, they wouldn't connect the missing matches with me and the school.

Then, when I thought they had forgotte, the fateful day came round and I took out the matches, hid them behind a big book, told my mother the book needed to go into school with me and off we went.

I must have been very calm. I don't remember worrying once I set off. I was driven to school, so must have looked okay all the way there. In I went, hiding the matches again once I was inside.

My plan was to wait until lunchtime break, when everyone would be out of the school and set fire to it then. I didn't want anyone to get hurt. It never occurred to me that the school wouldn't be empty, that the staff would still be inside and some children too.

When no one was looking, I sneaked back in, found my matches and looked for things to burn. I started with a big A2 sized sheet on a noticeboard. It burned well but the noticeboard didn't catch. Then, (oh reader, look the other way), I tried to burn some books. I felt very bad about them, but it was a means to an end and as they'd go up with the school anyway, I thought I might as well use them.

Then I ran out, into the playground, confident the school would be burned down by the time we had to go back in.

There's a blur after that. The school did not burn down, the fire was quickly put out and a full assembly was called. As they talked about what had happened and asked who had done it, my face told them all they needed to know and I was hauled off.

Sitting in the classroom, surrounded by teachers, all asking me how I did it, why I did it, what I had thought would happen. My distinct memory is of the kindly dinner lady looking at me from across the room, shaking her head sadly and saying to her friend that she'd thought I was such a nice little girl.

The teachers wouldn't believe that I had planned it all and acted alone. They simply wouldn't have it that I was capable. They also didn't see the bullying as a good enough reason. In my panic, after being asked over and over who else was helping me, I named a boy in my class. Ashley, I said, he helped me.

They were content with that. I didn't know Ashley, but they seemed happy to think he was the other one. I don't know how much trouble he got into, but the guilt of falsely naming him plagued me for years, long, long after any worry I might have had about trying to burn down the school. I'm sorry Ashley! :'(

The outcome was slightly unexpected. My parents were shocked but also ashamed they hadn't listened to me. The teachers may have felt some of the same, who can tell? The children were wary of me and slightly in awe. I don't remember getting bullied again after that.

I was grounded for a few weeks and didn't get to go on the school trip. Like a true aspie, when trip time came around, I'd forgotten about not being allowed and went to the teacher, in front of the class and asked why she hadn't given me the letter about it. She had to remind me, in public, why I wasn't going.

The day of the trip was fabulous. I got to stay with the younger class, with a lovely teacher who spoke nicely to them and gave them fun things to do. I spent the day drawing and writing stories and playing games. I remember wishing all my school days were like that one.

So, there we are, the beginnings of my own attempts to change my life when it refuses to change for me. I feel sure that I would always have been the sort of person to do strange things in response to life events, but this early, desperate experience contains all the hallmarks of my many misadventures since.

I planned, I was calculating, I was very calm. All of this as the end result of months of anxiety, nights spent lying awake, dreading going into school. It's an ice cold meltdown because you've gone through the fire of temper and stormy reactions, right to the calm within the storm where, finally, you can hear yourself think and plan what to do about it.

It's the same as a meltdown in that it holds a destructive quality which can seriously impact your life and others, but unlike the tradi-tional meltdown, however mad the plan, you feel like you're in con-trol.

I would like to reassure you, readers, that I haven't taken any violent or drastic action like this since. It was explained to me how many people would have been in the school if it had burned down and I was horrified at what might have been. It informed all future decisions in those two vital ways: never cause physical harm to someone and don't blame other people for your messes.

For those of you who plan their own salvation, I salute you. I know how it feels to be so desperate, you'll come out from under the blanket and take action. I also know that you'll have some understanding of how far I had to be pushed before I acted in this way.

For anyone who thinks I was a terrible person, look at me as I was then, a small child with no one to help me. I often look back and wish I could slip a hand through time and take the smaller version of mine when she was at her lowest ebb.

In our adult lives, we don't tend to set fire to things to make them go away, but we should be wary of the virtual blaze we cause by leaping into new decisions, without having full possession of the facts. I would never say don't do it - I still do it all the time myself. I would say, be careful *how* you do it, because you never know if you have missed something, or someone, in your planning. You may think you know all the answers, but there is always something you'll miss.

The most we can ever do is our best at any given time. Take charge, meltdown, hide under the blanket, cuddle the cat - do whatever it takes to get you through the hard times. Do that, always with an eye on yourself. There is no way for us to reach out through time to help ourselves, but you can reach out to yourself, now, as another person might and say,

'I know it's hard, we can get through this. Take my hand and I'll keep you company as we go.'

CHRISTMAS AND SPECIAL
OCCASION TRAUMA

I had to give this one its own section as Christmas, birthdays and other special occasions are a potential nightmare for aspies and their loved ones. The difference in routine, the need to meet other people, sometimes lots of them at a time, the expectation that the aspie will, on this occasion if no other, be sociable to people they don't like, is immense.

I love Christmas, but still find it difficult. I do not like my birthday! I like other people's birthdays better than my own. For my birthday, I would like everyone to give me the present of pretending it is just another day and maybe, sometime next week, we'll go out for a quiet meal somewhere and you can leave a present on the back seat of the car for me to open later, alone.

Yes, I do sound miserable. It's not meant that way, though. Special occasions come with people, presents, noise, excitement and one big, extra-super-sized dollop of STRESS. As aspies already feel stressed by a lot of situations, then it's no surprise that an occasion which combines numerous stress factors all in one go, is going to have more effect.

It's fine, though. It will pass. The secret is in making it possible for you and your aspie to enjoy the occasion in your own ways, so that if you have the choice, you can arrange the day how you please.

If you don't have the choice and are forced to go to cousin Nigel's wedding, then there are ways to cope with that too.

Be of good heart, readers, for special occasions, by their very nature, don't happen often. Luckily, this means that the aspie fireworks which usually accompany them don't happen too often either. Stand firm, put the kettle on and hide under the table if it gets really bad. It'll soon be another normal day with blessed routines back in place, you just have to keep your nerve until then.

AN ASPIE AT CHRISTMAS-TIME

Okay, this is often the big one for many families, aspie or not. Christmas can be a time of fraught emotions, high temper and stress caused by so many different things at once, you end up wondering if it's all worth it. The cosmic rule is that there must be at least one Christmas argument, and this can be like the single match in a box of fireworks.

Of course, there is the good side too. As I've mentioned before, I love Christmas - adore it in fact - but no matter how I love it, I'm still prone to the stresses of the season. What I've described could be any Christmas in a lot of homes, but imagine all these difficulties combined with the aspie mentality. If a normal day can stress you out in strange and unusual ways, then it's safe to say that Christmas is a front runner as a spectacular problem area.

When I was little, my mother and I would do the Christmas run-around, the one where you visit all the relatives you barely ever see and catch up. It's a good thing to do, a worthwhile way to touch base with them and show you care. If you live close enough, it's so much better than a card in the post. How we both hated it, though! The mental effort involved in going into all those different homes and being friendly and sociable with people we weren't close to anymore. We were still pleased to see them, it was just a supreme effort to be these bubbly personalities for hours on end. By the end of the day, home would seem like a glittering oasis, waiting to welcome us back to sanity.

Worse than this is the visiting you endure from other people. When they come to your door, carrying presents or cards and a wide smile, what can you do but roll out the bubbly personality again? Exept this time you have the uncertainty of how long they'll stay or what you should do with them while they're here. Everyone is expected to be sociable at Christmas, it's a standard response to the season. We are all suddenly supposed to *show* how much we care about each other, even if we don't really care at all.

What I find happens is, you show the caring to the people you don't really know anymore, then when it comes to displaying your emotions for the ones you do care about, it won't come out right.

You see, if you don't see someone much, it's easy to pretend for a little while that you've really enjoyed coming out and visiting them, or even welcoming them into your home. It can seem hard, but it's a limited-time experience. Once you're apart, you can relax again.

With people you do care about, they know you much better and can tell when you're pretending, or forcing it, or over-egging the pudding for the occasion. They can tell if your smile was pasted on just before you walked through the door. They can see the desperation in your eyes, except they'll translate it as anger or drama.

Also, with loved ones, even those you don't live with, you generally have to spend longer with them at Christmas. Even if it's just a visit, you'll usually take more time over it than with people you don't know so well. Which means, you have longer to mess it up and upset people - not that you often need more time to do this, of course.

The difficulty is in showing the correct emotions at the correct time. For heaven's sake! If only I could flick the switch that says 'show feelings', then this would be fine. I'm so busy avoiding eye contact with the present-giver that I don't have enough reaction space left over to show delight and often end up looking blank (for a change, ha-ha).

And then, if I could flick the emotion switch on Christmas day, would it be wise? What if I was completely honest and showed real emotion for each present, or relation, or my actual feelings on the belching over the Christmas dinner, or talking over the movies? Hmm, on reflection, it might be better to leave the reactions as they are. At least a blank face gives less offence than a face taking on a sudden likeness to a troll who was expecting goat and instead got new thermal underwear to keep him warm while he's loitering under the bridge.

It is definitely the little things that make Christmas difficult, though. You don't have to go through massive arguments to suffer from other people. All you need is constant interaction with them, in your home or theirs, with no proper excuse to leave and hide in your room. You have a situation at Christmas where it is not acceptable to hide, leave, not talk, drift off to the planet Nog or give monosyllabic answers to every question.

It's the time of year when it can be a blessing to be the one responsible for dinner. Yes, wrestling with a giant bird in the kitchen is preferable to sitting in the living room, talking to people. Being in charge of the food is also a wonderful excuse to regularly leave the room, so that you give the appearance of being sociable but don't have to stick around too much.

I would give two warnings here, though. Don't sound too sharp when you refuse offers of help, or you will give the game away that you prefer the kitchen to your guests. And for those of you who imbibe, *do not*, whatever you do, have a full glass of wine every time you're alone with the bottle.

If you do, you'll get progressively happier every time you return to the living room, but dinner will suffer and, so much worse than this, your inhibitions will pack their bags and have an overnight stay somewhere else. This leaves you free to tell your relatives that you don't see why they can't eat with their mouths shut, or say excuse me before leaning their woolly arms over your dinner, or ask you about your love life, or why we have to hear *that* story again, at the dinner table, over food.

The downside to not being able to imbibe is that you're stone cold sobre through the whole of the visit and can process every belch, mannerism, annoying habit, personality deficit or repetitive gesture your relatives make. It does also mean you're probably the only one still awake after dinner, which can be a blissful experience, especially if you manage to take charge of the TV controls before everyone nods off.

In my experience, if I can maintain a cool distance from my own irritations, I pass through the vale of antagonism to the hillock of hilarity. In other words, without the aid of alcohol, everything will become funny. This is great when it helps me to appear cheerful with people I want to slap, but not so great when you pass that stage and your sense of humour is the thing helping you get past your inhibitions. So, instead of alcohol making you tell it like it is, you end up joking about the bad habits going on around you. Oh yes, soooo funny. Funnier still when you see their faces change and they're forced to laugh, because it is Christmas after all.

Except, it doesn't stay funny for long - just long enough to make you look like a loon with no manners. Christmas, like any other time, shows how unacceptable it is to bring up the behaviour of others, no matter how bad it is. As always, aspies have to learn how to behave well in a normal world, while bearing up under the strain of other people's peculiarities. I've no idea why it's okay, for instance, for Aunty Gladys to ask me if I have a boyfriend every time she sees me, but it's not all right for me to ask her if she still isn't allowed in the bingo hall.

Readers, I did intend to offer solutions to Christmas stress, but all I seem to have done is outline the difficulties we might have this holiday season. I do apologise, I hadn't realised it was a problem without a solution. I can only say, do the whole thing in little bits as much as possible.

Like when I organise the food, take your opportunities to leave the room and rest. Think of it as a power rest, if you like, rather like a power nap without the sleep. Even if it's only a few seconds, take a deep breath and soak up the peace of the moment.

Try not to give in to any impulses which will come back to haunt you, like explaining exactly *why* Aunty Gladys isn't allowed in the bingo hall to those relatives who don't know the full story. I know, when you're under pressure, how tempting it is to pay it back to the people causing you trouble, but don't do it: usually they think they're being pleasant and making conversation and don't mean to drive you insane.

Take pleasure in the people you do want to see this season, even if you're seeing them online and not in real life. Friends come in all guises and you don't need to feel stuck with the real-life versions, who you have to let in the door because they saw you before you saw them. Some of your rest time could be spent with your online friends, a place of solace when your physical surroundings seem to be closing in to stamp on you with heavy boots.

If all else fails, do be rude and hide in your room. It's only you being difficult again, after all. Everyone knows how awkward you are, it shouldn't be a surprise. This should be your back up plan, though, as it isn't good to bail out completely and leave others to pick up the pieces.

Compromise, if you have family or a best beloved who will look out for you. Tell them to fill in the gaps with any visitors if you disappear for a while. Tell them you won't go missing for the full day, if you can help it. It's so much easier to re-enter the room if you know a kind soul has told a white lie on your behalf, as then people won't make a fuss over your absence or your reappearance.

All in all, readers, I do still love Christmas, but I'm not blind to the problems caused by being an anti-social, routine-loving aspie in the midst of fellowship and song. Do try to feel some of the wonder of the season, the glow of excitement or the contentment and peace of the dream of Christmas.

Don't try too hard to deal with it like everyone else. Whatever the time of year, or the occasion, you are still you and it will always be that way. Try to enjoy yourself and relax. You never know, this might be the year when everything almost goes to plan,
or when you don't care that it doesn't.

No matter what, hold fast to your blanket and look to your loved ones for help. Christmas only comes once a year, so sooner rather than later, it will all be back the way you want it to be.

ASPIES DON'T LIKE SURPRISES!

Interwoven in so many of my writings about aspergers has been the notion of aspie reactions to life, the universe and everything. It always seems to be reactions, have you noticed that? The aspie, in defence as usual. This is because we don't often expect the outcomes we're presented with, so we do end up defending ourselves against yet another surprise.

This is why aspies don't like surprises - every blooming day has them and they're very rarely nice. I don't mean that every day I open the post and I've won the Reader's Digest draw or there is a bunch of flowers from a secret admirer on the front step. Neither do I mean that people shower me with unexpected compliments or the cake turns out better than expected.

No, I mean the kind of surprises that are small enough to act like bullets, slipping through the mithril vest of aspergers and into the defenceless heart.

The sort of surprise that happens in conversations with people who should know better, where you get something wrong and they laugh at you. You like them and they like you so why did they laugh? That's a surprise. Or realising in the middle of the queue that you left your card at home and have 23 pence and a button to pay for the load of shopping already travelling along the conveyor - that's a surprise too. Or suddenly remembering the you're meant to be picking the kids up from school and you're already ten minutes late.

All these masquerade as surprises, dear reader. They pretend to be small and innocuous little surprises, the kind of things people brush off and say 'it doesn't matter', 'it's not important'. In the grand scheme, they aren't important, I can see that. I can even tell myself that at the time. In the region of the heart, where the nasty little beggars have found a way through, they do hurt and they do matter.

They are not surprises, they are little shocks.

I'm not talking about proper shocks, like the roof falling in or finding out the hard way there are loose wires in the plug. I mean little jolts, like when a cat gives you a warning bite or a toddler nips you in the neck. You won't die, you most likely won't even bruise and other people expect you to laugh it off.

The thing with surprises and shocks though is that they are unexpected and, with aspergers, quite frequent. A lot of the time you can be surprised simply because you had already worked out in your head how something would turn out. We have a naturally tendency to plan ahead, so we can organise ourselves and know what to do without having to stop everything and figure things out. When something goes wrong - or feels like it's gone wrong - it's an unwelcome surprise and it jars the whole operation, leaving you feeling slightly out of control.

And there is the key word here: not surprises, not shocks but Control. Aspies love to have control, it's a beautiful thing. I don't mean we all want to rule the world or even expect to be in charge (no thanks!), I mean that having control over what goes on around you makes it feel safe and helps you get through the day in one piece.

If you're feeling delicate but still need to go out into the world of lions and tigers and bears, you can plan ahead, plan it step by step, down to whatever detail you like. It's actually safer to plan it only to medium-density, as then you can leave room for little things to change and not feel worried when they do. However, accepting that little things can change is not the same as accepting surprises.

For instance, you need to get the car fixed at the garage. It's not a very good day but it has to be done. You take it in, knowing you can wait as it won't take long. You know how you'll be greeted, they'll take the keys, you'll sit down in the waiting room. There may be other people, the man might offer you a coffee, which you'll decline as you have no idea how to work the coffee machine. The TV may be on. There may not be a place to sit. You decide, before going in, whether or not you'll stay in the waiting room if there is nowhere to sit. You decide to keep your coat on as it can be cold in there and being nervous makes you shiver, so you don't want to shiver through cold as well.

There, all prepared and off we go.

You get to the garage and realise you left your glasses at home. You left wearing the prescription sunglasses. If you take them off, you can see but not well enough to focus properly or read anything. Plus, you have a tendency to scowl at things. If you keep them on, you look weird, sitting in the waiting room, wearing shades.

This unwelcome little surprise is shelved away. You cope with it, try to ignore it, sashay into the garage waiting room and give them the keys. Politely decline the coffee and turn round to sit down.

There is a space and it's opposite the TV. Now you can pretend to watch it while you sit there, regretting your glasses being at home. You accidentally sit on someone's coat. It's okay, it'll be fine. You smile at them, conscious you have a slightly zoned out expression without your glasses (yes, for those who know me, I have this expression with them too).

All is fine and then you need to sign for the car. You have another little shock, realising you can't see where you're meant to sign without putting the prescription sunglasses on. Do you guess and hope you don't sign the counter or put the sunglasses back on and look weird?

In this real-life scenario, I put them back on, waggling them at the chap behind the counter and explaining I had left my glasses at home. Of course he didn't care, I was worrying for nothing. It's always surprising to me how non-judgmental people can be when you're feeling vulnerable and then how callously cruel some will be when you least expect it.

Catastrophe averted, you take the keys and leave. It was all worry over nothing but that didn't stop you fretting for most of the time you were there.

This is the sort of surprise brought on by myself, by forgetting my glasses, but it shows how one quite small thing can impact on everything else. It also emphasises how tenuous that feeling of control can be. It doesn't take much for the control to feel like it's slipping, even when barely anything has changed. That sense of loss of control can change your whole perspective and make a so-so day a really difficult one.

Coming back to the surprises angle, the way most non-aspies encounter this hatred of surprise and change is when they want to do something with their beloved and find a brick wall in the way. This can range from wanting to go to the park on the 'wrong' day, to doing something special and exciting for a birthday, to wanting to make Christmas a day to remember (I'm going to cover aspies and Christmas as a separate post quite soon).

You notice how none of these things are done to hurt the aspie. The worst part is they are often done to make the aspie happy! So when it falls apart because the beloved reacts badly and hares off back to the safety of the computer, the non-aspie can feel very, very hurt and let down. It doesn't matter in that moment that they understand a lot of the aspergers behaviour: what matters is they, personally, planned something lovely and had it shoved back in their face.

I'm sorry, I can't make it better. Too often I've been the one who has had to bear surprises. Adult aspies will often try harder than children and young people to hide their horror of the unexpected. I will try to look forward to the unseen present in the wrapping paper. I'll try to summon enthusiasm for the day out when it's my usual day for something else. I will really, really try to look pleased when you spring a brilliant surprise on me, out of nowhere, when I thought you had just come for a coffee and a chat.

All too often, my true feelings and the true feelings of many an aspie, show in the face to such an extent I might as well just give in and shriek as I run off into my bedroom.

You see, even nice surprises are stressful, mainly because of two very important reasons:

1. It's a change from the routine and we have the routine sussed out

2. You expect an emotional reaction from *us* and are giving one *yourself*

I've covered how changing number 1 can impact on us, as the feeling of control slips away. Number 2 is even trickier.

I might love the present, you may have chosen the perfect gift, the most perfect, extraordinary, amazing gift. Then you wrapped it and gave it as a surprise. You watched me intently as I opened it. The pressure builds - a surprise, an audience, expectations, feelings, your eyes boring into my face, the need to show my emotions strongly, so you can see how I feel.

All of this overwhelms the gift itself and the moment of giving. I don't necessarily want to spoil it by being told what the gift is (though that may work for some aspies). It helps if I get a warning, though, something like, 'you'll like your gift, it's right up your street,' or 'don't worry, you will like it'. Nothing specific, you see, just reassurance.

You can watch me open it, but try not to sit forward on your seat, face alight, hands clasped together. Maybe chat a little to other people, or even to me. Maybe hold something in your hands so that I'm not your only focus. Have the TV on in the background, so I can see it out of the corner of my eye and not just have the drama of you, me and the present.

Make the opening and giving of the present something with an element of control to it. Ask me if I would like to open it now, let me know by your body language that you are relaxed and it's no big deal. Let me get myself comfortable; if necessary, let me leave the present and then open it later.

I've concentrated more on presents and the coping mechanisms in play there, but it can be applied to any surprise you need to share with your aspie. The main idea is in the aspie retaining control, or the feeling of control. If you have something shocking to tell them, don't lead up to it too gently. Let them know you have to tell them something they won't like, that is a shock. You can't always soften the blow but it really helps if you know a little of what type of thing is coming.

For the rest of it, for the hurt feelings as you and your idea/present/day out are rejected, just let it flow a little. You have probably been told, or gathered by now, that your aspie does not like surprises. Once you've got over your hurt feelings, reflect on the fact that it shouldn't really have been a surprise to you that your beloved was not pleased. Admit to yourself that you wanted to please your aspie, but were also pleasing yourself, by making it a surprise.

I realise that may read a little harshly, like a criticism. It is and it isn't. I know you do these things because you love us and want to please us. I also know your aspie will have made clear, by body language if not by word and deed, that they do not appreciate being surprised. Please, please respect this as much as possible and make allowances for it.

And if you really must give your aspie a delicious surprise, warn them beforehand. Yes, that sounds like a contradiction but it really isn't. Tell them you have a surprise for them. Their heart will sink, honestly it will. Follow it quickly by saying it's something you're sure they will like, then after that you can give them the surprise.

Like going to the garage, the shop, the school or out into the world in general, when it comes to feeling in control, preparation is everything. Then surprises can be absorbed and coped with and (don't tell anyone!), a little bit enjoyed.

Oh, and before I forget - don't worry about the super-duper special present we seemed so lacklustre about. We actually love it, it really is the best thing ever. We'll go online and tell everybody what a great person you are for knowing us so well. We won't shut up about it. And in bed that night, we'll think about it and smile, because we know you love us so much. And eventually, we'll tell you how much we liked it. You just have to be patient. Annoying, I know, but everything moves at its own speed and aspies are no different.

LOGICAL THINKING

Oh dear, the trouble an aspie can get into with logical thinking. You see, we're used to watching what we say and how we express our thoughts and feelings as, so often, other people don't understand us. But when something is logical, then it is what it is and our normal filtering system is not activated. Whatever we see as logical will come spilling out, expressed in blunt terms because we all know it must be true.

And then, the room is silent once more and you see the shocked faces and the hurt expressions. Frankly, at this point, I do often feel annoyed. I mean, bad enough when I say something accidentally hurtful, but for you all to be shocked when I state the obvious? Can I do nothing right?

Apparently, other people don't always see things as logically as I do myself. This is still a mystery to me as I don't know how they can miss the obvious so easily. It also makes it seem more important for me to explain it to them and state the logic, so they can keep up.

Except, you then have a repeat of the situation above and are accused of being unkind and unfeeling. How annoying! Why do people have to be so touchy anyway?

It's made all the worse by logic being something we aspies find easier to understand than most other things. Compared to the confusion of life and its variety of tricks, logic is like an oasis we can trudge towards, gleaming ahead of us with the promise of sustenance. We don't need to try to understand logic, there are no hidden trapdoors, there is no pot of steaming oil waiting to fall. Logic is what it says it is and we love it.

So, to pained non-aspies everywhere, I make no apologies for this one. Please try to see how much we love logic and how it's a compliment that we share it with you. We're only trying to help and we really can't be held responsible if your non-aspie brains can't see the obvious thing right in front of you. Aren't you pleased we're there to point it out for you, so you don't miss it?

LOGIC AND THE ASPIE POINT OF VIEW

I want to talk about aspergers and logic, or how aspies use facts to explain life and also to explain themselves.

Super-logic could describe what happens when you try to argue with a calm aspie. When an aspie is calm and in possession of the facts, there is no point in even opening your mouth. It won't matter what you say, you will be proved wrong.

I say this in all humility, believe it or not. I'm just being logical. I know that it's often me who gets worked up, takes things the wrong way and seems to provoke confrontations in the most unexpected situations. I just mean that when I'm actually *right* about something, it's no good you going and getting upset about it.

I've had many conversations with people who expect to come out as being right. They are used to me being a dithery, confused-face who will pause in the middle of a conversation while I play it back to see what was said. Yes, I admit it, I can often be an infuriating person to talk to as I forget what you've said, almost always forget what I've said too and then can't remember what we were talking about.

How incensing it must be, then, to have an argument with me and suddenly find my brain has tripped some kind of robot-overlord switch where I know all the facts and can disprove your point of view again and again.

Oh dear, the times this has happened and a nice conversation has turned bitter. You see, as aspies, we're used to being wrong about things and usually take it with good grace (unlike some non-aspies, I may say). We're used to giving the little smile, or the shrug and apologising.

When we know what we're talking about, though, there's no stopping us. Similar to the obsessions that carry us along, knowledge, once stored, is there forever and if we access it at the right time and place, we then access the whole of it. And we know it's true.

So in an argument (and it always becomes an argument), don't try to get us to back down if we know something. We read it, we heard it, we watched it, we stored it and now we're telling you about it. Whatever it is, it probably disproves the thing you were talking about. Your point of view is irrelevant because it came up against the solid wall of the Known Fact.

At this point, the aspie can be at their most annoying. Yes, even more annoying than when they ignore you, or make that weird sound on the escalator. Aspies when they're being eccentric or zoned out are bad enough: aspies who are being *in the right* are unbearable. Truly awful.

Sometimes, when I'm in the middle of proving whatever point it is, I catch sight of the whole situation from the outside. One of those rare moments of insight sneak up on me and I'm able to see it all as if I'm watching it.

If this happens, I can see that I'm being obnoxious. I can see the other person is inflamed and probably upset. I can understand how I look and sound, this monolith of logic, repeating the right facts, carrying on regardless.

You know what? The pull of logic is so strong that even when I have these moments of insight and realise I'm acting like a giant, phlegmy boil on the backside of humanity, even then I still say to myself, 'It can't be helped, I'm right.'

It sounds horrible, doesn't it? I've made myself and other aspies sound as if we couldn't care less that you feel so upset you don't know whether to cry or start throwing Grandma's crockery. It's not like that, though. Honest.

You see, things are what they are. Some things, lots of things, are confusing and unknowable. Other things are transitory pieces of knowledge, kept for a little while then set free. There are so many things to know and learn, we just can't keep track of them all.

But, if we grasp a hold of something and do keep it, then it's *ours*. We know it, we know it so much that we can *feel* it. It belongs to us and becomes part of us! The triumph of the gold-coloured Fact, the wonderful shine, the lustre, the feeling that here, right in our hand, we have something that we are certain is correct.

So, if that Fact comes up later, perhaps years later, in a conversation, we whip it out so that it can shine in the sunlight. We know it, we share it with you. If it doesn't fit what you know, then that's a shame because we know it's true, which is why we told you about it.

If you are determined to carry on the conversation as if our lustrous Fact didn't matter, then what else are we to do but draw your attention to it again? After all, it's important, because it's true. If you had listened properly, then you would know by now. We'll tell you again.

Why you might get worked up or upset is one of those little mysteries. As I said, we also get upset over things but are used to being wrong, so perhaps it's less of a trial to us. Now that we are right, there's no need to be upset. Just listen and you'll find out what we mean.

This can go on indefinitely, Readers. I know that most of you will walk away or scream first, then walk away. Mostly, these arguments won't get as far as Grandma's crockery. Sometimes they will. They can become those silly rows that end up in life-changing drama.

The trouble is, an aspie in the right, with the Facts to hand, is an immovable object. They have the Facts, you do not. They present you with the Facts, you ignore them. Repeat as necessary.

The carelessness with feelings which seems to accompany this ritual is not really intentional. It seems to be a by-product of firmly, stoically, repeating what you know in the middle of an illogical conversation. The conversation is illogical because it is failing to recognise the aspie's Fact as truth. And so on.

The aspie themselves may also get upset but that won't make the Fact any less true. The aspie might be the one to leave, to do the dramatic flounce out of the room, door whallopped against the wall, picture tumbling to the ground, feet on the stairs as the sound of a distant crash hails the meeting of temper and book shelf.

None of that matters, either. If the conversation is revisited, as a way of soothing and reintroducing peace, the Fact will still be true and had better be avoided.

Now, look at all that again and imagine how this plays out if the Fact isn't true. What happens then? What if the aspie is wrong or the Fact is old news, out of date and reinvented since learned?

That's the tricky part because if the aspie knew this, they'd back down. But it's no good just telling them and expecting it all to be over. Like all the other information that didn't make the transition into shining Fact, your new fact is small and easily lost. It isn't to be trusted, not like the one the aspie knows.

You can only replace the original knowledge in another time and place, by coming at it from a different angle. Is it important that the truth be known? If it is, then try and do it gently and with subtlety. If it isn't important, it's up to you whether you shy away or bring it up again.

Logic is such a funny thing. It can give aspies strength as it doesn't rely on feelings, expressions, learned behaviour, accepted humour or any of the facets of a troubling world. Logic is of itself, a clearly-defined creature with limitations you can spell out.

As such, Logic is smooth, stress-free, like a cool breeze on a hot day. You can turn your face into it and smile, knowing there won't be any rough edges or surprise corners to make you think again. Logic is a friend who can be trusted.

It appeals to the obsessive side of the aspie to believe in Logic, because if something is so utterly trustworthy, then it can be controlled. It's only the unpredictable side of life you have to watch out for.

In an argument, if Logic, in the shape of known facts, is under attack, then so is the aspie's feeling of control and safety. We know this Fact is true, truth is safety. You say it isn't true, but I won't back down. You can't take my safety away from me without a fight!

This isn't the thought process, but it is the feeling that comes with it.

Logic in the aspie world can be likened to the characters in the Wizard of Oz. No, I'm not suggesting we all trip off down the yellow brick road. That would be silly. It would mean leaving the computer, not having access to a kettle and biscuits and also seems to require linking arms with strangers, dancing in public and raising your voice high enough to be heard when you sing.

What does Logic have to do with this strange reflection of reality, in Dorothy's trip to Oz? Well, at the end of the story, Dorothy and her friends learn that what they thought they knew was always wrong. The Scarecrow could be clever, the Lion could be brave, the Woodsman had a heart and Dorothy always had the power to go home.

Would they have agreed with that at the start of the film? No. Did it mean they were stupid or wrong to set off on their journey, in full and certain belief that they could reach their destination? No, of course not, because without the journey they would never have discovered the real truth.

Every aspie, even the ones with unassailable Facts, is travelling that same journey. We think we move along this way, for *that* purpose. What we are really doing is running through life, trying to learn enough along the way to do what needs to be done. We want to be bigger, better people, with more knowledge, a better understanding of others and the courage to keep facing the world.

We want to be able to find our way home and are always looking to other people to show us the answer to this and our other questions.

Aspies, like everyone, have the answers already inside them. It's logical to look outside and think we can learn the Facts there and there alone. What we aspies have to do, and what you best-beloveds must help us to do, is to look within and trust ourselves enough so that we don't need logic all the time.

It doesn't have to make sense to be true. It doesn't have to be logical to feel right. The facts aren't always what they seem, because they cannot stand alone, they must measure up to the world around them.

As aspies, we must learn to yield ourselves to fortune and other people. Yes, I'm saying we need to learn how to link arms with strangers and dance in public. Not literally, perhaps, but the need to connect is what saves us from the kind of rigid thinking that makes logic the king of every conversation.

For even aspies like me, who have random tattooed on their hard drives, are also slaves to logic. I believe, so many times, that I must do *this* to get *that*. I believe that life follows a pattern and if I learn the pattern then I'll know about life.

Through writing this blog and re-discovering the many ways my brain and heart can work together, I see there are more paths to knowledge than the one I follow. I need to make my own way, trust instincts before facts, be my own person first and a traveller second.

Readers, I hope you can join me and my fellow aspies as we learn that logic, knowledge, facts aren't always the answer. Be there to pick up the pieces when we learn we got it wrong. It can be terrible when logic fails you, when you feel deserted by a reliable friend.

Try not to notice that we got it wrong and just help us get started again. Pick up those apples, put them back in the basket and off we go again. It'll be all right, if only you are there too.

LITERALLY?

Literally? Figuratively? Rhetorically? When it comes to 'lys' there are lots and they all have their attractions. For me, though, Literally is the one I am drawn to the most. Literally gets me and I get Literally. We know where we're both coming from.

I have this problem with other 'lys'. They always seem to be trying to catch me out and make me look stupid. You can be having a nice chat with someone and they tell you something shocking. You react and they laugh - they didn't mean it literally! You laugh too, most of the time. Just sometimes, you feel hurt. Not by them, don't get me wrong. They hardly ever mean it unkindly. By yourself. Hurt by yourself - again.

Why can't I tell when someone is being rhetorical? Why can't I tell the difference? I mean, I can do most things in life; I don't need looking after. I function as an almost-normal human bean, for heaven's sake! And I'm not so literal that I don't know the difference between being told to take a running jump and actually doing it.

The problem is, I'm *just* literal enough to make life difficult. It all comes down to belief.

If someone tells you something outrageous, like they want you to go jump off a cliff, you can tell it's a cliche, and is not (usually) meant literally. Sometimes what they say can be audacious and so you train yourself to question it. As a child, you don't have the audacity filter though.

As a child, if someone had told me to jump off a cliff, I would have refused but I would suspect they really wanted me to do it. But other, slightly less audacious things, got right past me.

I had an auntie who was always on a diet. She told me once, in all seriousness (I thought) that when she was really ready to lose weight, she would come to our house and live in a cage in our living room, and I could feed her food through the bars, so that she could never over-eat. Yes, it was a joke and also a descriptive way of telling me she thought it was almost impossible to lose weight.

I spent weeks, if not months, asking her when she was coming to live at our house in the cage. Eventually, my mother told me my auntie hadn't meant it. I was flabbergasted! So, why did she say it? I asked. It was a joke, I was told.

Then, you relay the idea of a joke past yourself a few times. I was only 8 but I knew a joke was meant to be funny and when something is funny, you laugh. I remembered my auntie laughing every time I asked her when she was going to live in the cage - so I realised then that she had found the joke funny. I also realised I hadn't, because it hadn't been a joke to *me*. I was upset about it. I was also annoyed - how in heck was she ever going to lose weight then? Did she not care about it anymore? (You see, even though the cage idea had been a joke, it still hadn't occurred to me there was any other way for my auntie to lose weight as she told me she had tried Everything).

It's at this point that we aspies, girls or boys, start to distrust humour. When jokes and laughings and happy hilarity enjoyed by others has tripped us and made us fall flat on our faces (sometimes literally, school is a cruel place), you start to think you don't like jokes. I actually still don't like jokes. I LOVE humour and comedy, I love subtle innuendo and slapstick. And I like puns, because they're using words I know in a different way, so you know they're not going to bite you on the bum. I don't like the kind of joke that pretends to be real, though.

I guess what I really don't like is the joke being at my expense. Not in the way of friends teasing you, or laughing when the cat eats your chicken - all that is fine. But not when your aspie-ness has reared its head, yet again, and singled you out as a joke-free zone.

I think the real problem is, when being literal and being truthful, all blend together with how people present themselves. An aspergers adult presents themselves they way they have learned is best for the world to understand them, not shout at them, not prod them with sticks and not question their sanity.

It's other adults I have most problems with. Most people, kind or unkind, don't say what they mean. I do wish they would. I much prefer grumpy sour-pusses who spit out the truth, than smiling assassins who act as if they're your friend, speak as if they are and pretend an interest in you, then drop you as soon as they feel like it. If you are in dire need and your life is spiraling out of sight into the toilet bowl, it's always the grumpy sour-pusses who turn up at your door with a pot roast and that all-important question: Tell me what you need.

Not to worry, though, as making and keeping friends is something an aspergers person can be good at - in the longer term. In the short term, our awkward way with strangers and our easy way of accidentally insulting people, can lose us the type of people who value the way something is said, rather than the meaning behind the words.

In the longer term, our stable of friends tends to consist of the kinder, more accepting types who make the world a better place, as well as the grumpy sour-pusses who exclaim 'What do you mean, fat?!' when we've said the wrong thing, so it all gets straightened out.

And then there are the other aspies. Yes, you know who you are. How easy it is to be friends with an aspie. They may get the wrong end of the stick and feel briefly insulted sometimes, but then they doubt themselves, replay it and decide we probably meant something else. Or they ask you to say *exactly* what you mean - that is so useful! Also, other aspies have been dealt many unkindnesses and so they tend to want to be nice to other people, as they know how it feels to be hurt by those words spoken flippantly by the general normality.

Literally, it can be hard to make friends and influence people. We're not so much separated by a common language as by a common misconception, that all humans are basically the same. Actually, we're not, on any level, be it literally, philosophically or even genetically. We may come from the same dna sample dropped into Mother Nature's green-goo-stew, but that's where it ends.

And believe me when I say, it's good to be different. Just, for heaven's sake, say what you *mean*!

FRIENDS, FAMILY & BEST-BELOVEDS

This section of the book is sent with love to the family, friends and best beloveds of aspies everywhere. So many times, their compassion and efforts to understand are swiped off the table and left, broken, on the floor. I want you to know, to really *see*, how important you are to us and how we couldn't do it without you.

Or at least, perhaps we could do it without you, but we wouldn't be the same people.

These posts were amongst the easiest and most difficult to write. Easy because they are so familiar and involve many situations I've been through myself. And difficult because I had to face the side of my Aspergers which makes me unkind, hard to live with, hurtful and generally irritating.

I had to grit my teeth as I wrote some of it and, like many times when writing my blog, tears fell as I typed. Sometimes, I come away from the blog and feel I've opened a door into the past and stepped through; other times I see my own future and it terrifies me. This is why I know our families and friends are the people who carry us along, even when we don't deserve the help.

I hope these chapters will make you feel a little less alone when the walls shake and you wonder why you keep on doing this. And for all the other times, when the aspie is only being a small tick instead of a giant gnat, at least you may be able to resist the urge to swat them by burying your head in this book.

LIVING WITH AN ASPIE

Oh dear, how often must the non-aspie have thought, 'I can't do this anymore. It's like I'm going mad, nothing makes sense!' I understand. It's hard enough when you are the aspie in question, so I can imagine it must be impossible at times to cope with an aspie from the outside.

Things which have no meaning are important in the aspie world. Noises the non-aspie has never even noticed are magnified and become an unreasonable stress to the aspie. Little routines, recognised by the non-aspie. seem to hold the key to the day's happiness. How can the toast being the right colour have a bearing on a person's emotional health? What does it matter which spoon you use to eat your cereal?

So many mysteries, so many ways to drive the aspie mad when, it seems, it should be the non-aspie who gets in the van and goes off to happy land. After all, what better way to push someone off the brink than by dancing along it beside them?

I think a word that must often rise up between the aspie and non-aspie is exasperation, from both sides. The non-aspie looks at their beloved and thinks, 'Why does it have to be done this way? Why can't I whistle while I make my tea? Why do you have to have things your own way all the time?' The normally patient non-aspie can be pushed to a point of temper that creates damaging arguments or unhappy atmospheres.

From the aspie point of view, it's logical (isn't it always?). They have made it clear, lots of times, which way things need to be done. It's always been all right before, the best beloved was happy to make sure they didn't use the wrong spoon. They never minded the wasted slices of toast before. Why does it suddenly matter today? And why, when they know it infuriates you, do they have to whistle all the time? It's not as if anyone enjoys listening to it, only the whistler is ever happy, not the whistlee.

The aspie may be a supremely aggravating person to live with, for many reasons, but they have their ways and it can seem illogical and upsetting to them if the non-aspie suddenly decides not to suffer those ways, or play along with them. Routine comes in many different guises, and one of those is the behaviour of your nearest and dearest. If that behaviour changes, for no obvious reason, how confusing and exasperating it can be.

Now, I must pause here, in defence of the non-aspie. Your behaviour may change and, to the aspie, there is no obvious reason, but we all know how obvious some things have to be before the aspie notices them. They haven't noticed you are tired this morning, or feeling ill. They haven't remembered you had an argument with your sister yesterday, or that you still need painkillers for a sprained ankle.

Yes, they know you may be about to lose your job; that was old news from last month. It wouldn't occur to them you were lying awake, thinking about it, worrying over it. That's the aspie seeming cold and uncaring again. In reality, the imminent job loss has been thought over, worried about, cared about, all at the time you discussed it and a little while after. Now, weeks later, there are lots of other things that need attention and as you didn't come up to the aspie and say you were upset about it, then how are they to know?

You see, the non-aspie is as mysterious and annoying as the aspie. Their little ways, which seem to be accepted as normal by so many people, often make no sense in the aspergers universe. Why does the housework have to be done before you go out? There's plenty of time when you get back. Why do you need to have a routine for the unimportant things in life, like the shopping, ironing, going to the hairdresser? Can't you just do them when they need to be done?

221

Why can't you apply for that great job in the paper? We aspies *know* you can do it, we see the qualities you have that make you perfect for it. Why do you have to concentrate on the physical skills that are lacking, instead of shooting off to see if you can do it, before deciding you can't? Why does it always have to be based on a practical reason?

In the aspie world, full of colour, explosions of sound, familiar things making comforting feelings, distractions leading to intense difficulty, or bringing us to a new understanding of life: in this world, doing things because it's the way they should be done makes no sense. Aspies, though creatures of habit, are also creatures of the moment. We forget it's Wednesday, forget the appointment, forget what was supposed to be for lunch today.

We remember that dream we woke from at 3am, the one that would make a great mosaic if we can only find the right pieces. Or we remember the grand plan, that will make all other grand plans meaningless. Or we wake up feeling like soggy bark, mulching down into the forest floor, good for nothing and certainly not able to go out and meet life's routines.

This is where we can meet, non-aspies and aspies alike. We know why we want to do a certain thing, even if the reason is a tenuous emotional connection. The toast has to be *just so,* the spoon has to be mine, because I feel better if it is that way. That is my reason. And if I feel better, the day is better.

So, when a non-aspie is exasperated again in the face of trying to make the aspie see that another thing is important, when the aspie only sees it as boring, practical stuff that has no place in their universe, **try explaining why it's important**.

If you, as the non-aspie, were to say, 'I need to do the housework before we go out because it makes me feel good and I can enjoy the day,' then we'll understand. What so often gets said instead is, 'The housework needs to be done before we go out.'

The word 'need' doesn't compute in this scenario. The house will not fall down, you will not be dragged out and arrested if the housework stays undone. What's the need? Why are you delaying our day out for that? Don't you care? How did I end up with someone who would rather do housework than spend the day with me?

Explanations are key. The non-aspie will very likely be better at verbal explanations than the aspie. The routines loved by the aspie will have been explained by actions more than explanation - in other words, the best beloved will have found out which is the wrong spoon the hard way! They will have learned what to do and what not to do by the aspie's reaction, rather than a calm discussion.

So, although the aspie may not have explained in the conventional sense, it doesn't mean the non-aspie can't use normal words and conversation to explain their feelings. It's as simple as getting the aspie's attention (cough) and telling them how you feel. No, I do not mean by saying, 'You're driving me insane today!' I mean telling the aspie, 'I need to do this because-'.

I'll end there for today, as I feel exhausted at the idea of all that unnecessary housework. I'll be re-visiting the concept of aspies and non-aspies living together in future posts, as I know it's one of the major hurdles we all face.

For now, I'll leave you with the promise that we can live together, even if we have to learn new ways of doing things. Hang in there, walk carefully, listen to each other.

And non-aspies, please, if your aspie has taken the trouble to say they think you can do a certain thing, consider the fact that they may see in you this bright and special person that the rest of the world has missed. Have another look at that big opportunity you think you can't do. Take the aspie at their word and see if there is a part of you that comes alive by being seen through the aspie-lens. You'd be amazed how wonderful everything can look with the right focus.

CHAOS IN THE HOME

Now for once I'm not talking about chaotic relationships or chaotic emotional meltdowns - though it's all linked. No, today I'm talking about a *physical* chaos, the scene that meets you when you walk in my home.

Let me be clear: I've never been tidy. Obsessive, yes. able to organise Stuff, most certainly. More than able to see other people's mess, unfortunately a definite yes. How about able to see my own mess, organise myself and keep it all clean and tidy? Erm, am I alone in this **No**?

I am better than I used to be. You no longer fall over last week's shopping bags as you walk through the door. There is a whole floor in the living room, rather than a path through to the sofas. You can tell my carpets are not collie-coloured.

I shop better and am less likely to find we have no milk in the morning. This does mean I'm back in Tesco at 11pm the night before, buying the milk, but this is a step forward from not realising until the next day. When RT teen goes to college, I have a packed lunch for him, unlike when he was little and we dashed to the shop for his lunch before school.

I *see* more of my mess and clutter, though this tends to depress me rather than making me tidy up more.

Now, to anyone out there who is already organised and tidy, big whoop to you, but please don't think I just need to pick up after myself and it'll all be solved. And don't assume that a big clear out, by me or brave volunteers, will result in the problem being sorted, once and for all. It doesn't work like that.

It kind of works like the rest of life, in that I see what I need to see. If I fall flat on my face, I'll move the box. If I only brush my leg against it every time I walk past, I will eventually move the box when the irritation gets too big too ignore. If the box is tucked out of the way and I never fall over it or touch it, then it has a good chance of becoming a solid, upstanding member of our family. If the box has any kind of soft or level surface, it will also become a much-loved cat bed.

The same applies to anything really. If it isn't in the way, it tends to stay where it lands. If it's comfy or interesting, the cats will always take an interest in it, ensuring it blends even more into the background. It will become part of the landscape and no longer an intruder.

I don't intend it to be this way. Believe me when I say, I have good intentions and always plan to have things in order, especially if some event is coming up, like birthdays or Christmas. And I do have a go, usually clearing and cleaning the places that are most public or have been cleared and cleaned already. So the already bearable places become more so, while the dark pits waiting for unwary visitors develop more of an atmosphere.

I've tried to follow routines and either forget to do them or life gets busier and I think I'll catch up tomorrow. Sound familiar? And there is always, without doubt, something better and more interesting I can be doing than shining the mirror or tidying the last birthday card so that we can put up the Christmas ones.

I should point out that you're quite safe to eat and drink here. The kitchen may be no more organised than the rest of the house, but thanks to me being a semi-obsessive handwasher and surface washer, you won't catch anything nasty if I cook for you.

I can hear the tidies amongst you wondering why I can't extend a little of this obsession to the rest of the house. Hmm, I've wondered that myself. I guess it's all about focus. I need to serve food in a clean area, so it is cleaned. The clutter and dust elsewhere is not in my direct path, be it a physical path or a mental one, so it doesn't need to be moved. If it doesn't need to be moved, then somewhere along the line my brain decides it doesn't need to be seen either. Why waste your attention on things that don't need it?

Readers, one of these days, possibly during some kind of long, drawn out, emotional episode, I may clean the whole house. It may happen. I do tend to think that some massive cosmic shift would have to occur for me to do it, but who knows? Perhaps I'm just a very slow mover, drifting like the continents as the years pass, each room becoming a little better but so slowly you can't see it with the naked eye.

I know from old photographs that things have improved. Now when you look, you can see which part of the picture has the cat in it. But there's still a way to go.

Don't judge me, readers, I do try; I just don't try often enough or with any great enthusiasm. And to fellow aspies, I do understand that it's not all mess or clutter; it is Stuff. Some of it is great Stuff too.

Be assured, aspie or non-aspie, that the chaotic realm you enter is a complete reflection of the person who lives there, no matter what they say. Perhaps this is why I've improved a little, as for years I denied the mess had anything to do with my internal chaos. As my own chaos receded, or developed a personality I could live with, so the external noise fell away and I was able to do more to make my home a safe place to cross floors.

In time, and with the help of IT teen's love for money, I hope to make all the corners of my home fit for human visitation. Yes, even the most aspie corners, the ones where dark shapes seem to move at night and little voices have started to talk to one another.

I'm determined that, at some stage, in the future, possibly next week, I'll get organised and finally tame the chaos in my home.

Whether it stays tame is another matter, but my intentions, as always, are good. Honest.

THE ROMANTIC ASPIE

No, don't get excited, I'm not about to declare my undying troth to someone or tell you all to buy hats for the wedding. I just think I've put it off long enough.

Yes, readers, I've been putting off writing about the romantic aspie. Well, is that the right phrase? Are other aspies more romantic than I am? I remember birthdays (or at least the month of the birthday) and Christmas is full of presents, but I'm not very good at the hearts and flowers.

I'm also not very sure how to present this subject to you, as myself and romance are not happy bedfellows, if you'll forgive the pun. As with so many relationships, the romantic side of things is complicated by many factors, mostly originating from me, which make getting to know other people and sustaining a relationship problematic at best.

In other words, aspies can be their own worst enemies.

At this stage in my life I forgive myself and other aspies for this. For many years I berated myself for not behaving properly or not being the kind of person who could be normal enough to make love happen. I had felt like this for most of my adult life, from before I had my first boyfriend and, if I'm honest, when I was married too.

It's a dimension of feeling left out, that sinking sensation we are all so familiar with where you are with people who are meant to love you but you feel like you wandered into the wrong life somehow. That feeling of disconnect, often wavering about at the edges of your life, comes through fully in a relationship because you are forced to face, head on, so many of your regular difficulties and phobias.

For instance, if you have a relationship with someone, you are meant to talk to them about your feelings, or at least show them how you feel. Our families are used to us either saying the wrong thing or sharing the bad feelings more often than the good, but with a new person we try harder to be what is expected.

So, you quite like a person and feel you could be together: what do you do next? Potentially, you are honest with them and tell them how you feel. Sadly, and more likely, you will either tell them what you think they want to hear - as you know romance is meant to be loving and supportive - or you don't share how you are feeling because it's private, even though it directly involves them.

Supposing your new best beloved can push past this, or has a very thick skin and you reach the next level of them wanting a commitment from you. Really? Commitment?? With another person besides yourself?

This one is only ever going to happen if the aspie decides it is. Seriously, it is a terrifying concept, for another person to expect you to commit to them, be responsible for them, every single day for the foreseeable future. (There may be aspies out there who are *not* commitment-phobes. If so, I apologise, this is from my personal point of view).

This is often the stage where a settled and more stable aspie would back off a little and say they wanted to take things a little slower. For those of us who panic, this is the part we do whatever it takes to make the other person back off and stop being so damn scary all of a sudden!

Trying to revert to a friendship stage in the middle of a romantic relationship seems like a soft way of showing your new beloved that you don't want to commit yet. It feels safer to push them away, just a little, and go back to the non-scary phase of being friends, having a good time and not expecting life to suddenly come together in a brutal melding of minds reminiscent of a giant squid attack.

To the other person, what on earth are they meant to think when the aspie wants to be friends again? That they are a vile excuse for a love match? That they smell? That they did or said something so horrendous their partner was put off for life? That if they try harder, they can make it work and undo whatever it was they did?

To the aspie, still revelling in the relief of being just friends again, all this angst is secondary to getting back to how we were before. There's no need for talking about feelings and stuff like that because now we can be happy friends again.

The aspie will probably become charming, putting in the effort to make this new phase work and pretending not to notice their partner's hurt feelings or confusion.

If an ultimatum is reached, of the new partner wanting a proper explanation of the strange behaviour, most likely the relationship will end. This is too full-on for aspies, who need to back away and hide, not become embroiled in the many perplexing layers of other people's feelings.

Enter even more confusion for the now-ex partner, who wonders afresh what they did to make all this happen. They will probably relive the relationship, looking for the cracks and seeing none. It might occur to them that the aspie was behaving oddly, but whether or not they know the aspie *is* an aspie, they must already have accepted the odd behaviours as part and parcel of their beloved to have even moved on to the next stage.

They will have asked for an explanation and, mostly, received none. The aspie will probably blame themselves, which is true, without giving any background as to why they became so uncomfortable so quickly.

The now-ex will either go on their way, putting it down to experience or have another go and accept the friendship terms after all, hoping that the future will bring them closer together and the relationship can flourish once more.

In a normal, sensible world, the relationship would have a chance of flourishing, but in the aspie world, if no real depth of explanation and understanding is reached, then they are doomed to repeat the cycle of potential relationships heaving to and fro between new beginnings and away from commitment.

Even if the aspie explains everything, lays it all out and shows their possible life partner the way they feel, why they feel it, what goes wrong, what feels wrong, what can be done...if all of this is done, it can still end in tears, simply because other people do not understand the depth of feeling in an aspie.

The potential partner cannot see why an aspie might cope quite well with life in general, only showing odd little ways now and then, but not be able to do the same with a proper relationship. It doesn't make sense to them. Why should an aspie face work every day and survive, but not be able to face a loving, supportive relationship?

Well, in work you are not yourself, you are the working person, the facade of the real you, the whatever-it-takes to make it through to the end of the day. In a relationship, you cannot and should not do that, so if the aspie is not happy and committed to another person, they have to put forward a facade for the relationship, just like they do for work.

It's very hard to be yourself the whole time, you see, as your whole self is used to being hidden away from the world, even from your own family. So for another person to want to share that, on a full-time basis, it just feels exhausting.

It comes down to what your partner expects of you. On top of any other difficulties you may have in romantic relationships, I think the expectations of the other person are the most harrowing. It's hard enough to commit to a relationship in the first place, despite all your phobias and problems dealing with other people, without also having to face the other person wanting a response from you, every time you are together.

I know I make it all sound like such hard work - and it is! I won't deny it, not on here anyway. I speak for myself and other aspies who have problems in this area. We will all react slightly differently, will all have the areas that cause us most stress, but the over-riding concern will always, always be our response to the other person in the relationship.

If we can get past the need to present ourselves and move forward into some kind of honesty, then the relationship may stand a chance. If we can put aside our misgivings at letting another person so far into our lives, then we can, perhaps, begin to relax.

If we don't feel able to do these things and the other person needs more from us than we can give at any one time, then we will probably retreat and close down the barriers again. Better safe than sorry, you see. Safe from any harm, no matter the good intentions behind that harm.

It always comes down to how we *feel*. Words, actions, plans, attraction, meeting of minds, it's all secondary to how we feel and whether we can cope with those feelings. After so many years of doing our best to cope with all of life, we don't want to have to cope at home too. Our safe place, that central feeling within us, is sacred and if we feel it is in danger, then we'll do what we have to and make it safe again.

It's sad to write all this, readers, just because so much of it is very familiar to me. I hope it isn't familiar to you, aspie or non-aspie. I hope you sit now, with your best beloved and wonder what I'm talking about.

I hope you can feel like you're in your safe place, even when another person is there with you. Or better still, that they are your safe place.

IT'S JUST THAT I DON'T CARE...

Now, come on, aspies, if you were all being brutally, exquisitely honest, how many times have you been tempted to respond with, 'I don't care how you feel, do what you like.' Insert other suitable words instead of feel, such as cry, or behave, or anything that other people do and expect a response for and away you go.

The emotional detach can be a wonderful thing, if you happen to be in the middle of a hurtful situation and there is no fast way out. This ability to disconnect and feel only the soothing waves of placid emotion, or to feel a numbness, a cosy blankness inside, it can be a life-saver - perhaps literally.

It's not that we are depressed, though it maybe sounds like that. It's more fundamental: it is a retreat into an inner place that is untouched by the stupendously irritating world of emotions. We are there, you are outside and you are not getting in.

This is an extreme reaction, often to a series of smaller events or one big one, where the aspie drifts away. It's a quiet meltdown, an unnoticed one. It is a leaving behind of the worries of the day and retreating to somewhere else.

But in the middle of this serenity, which can be so good for us, is the other side of the coin. What happens when this wonderful calm becomes a disinterest in someone else's feelings or situation? This is where I need you to read this honestly and not tut to yourself about what a horror I am and how you would never do that.

It's the old lack of empathy argument at work. Let's look at it like that, from the **non-aspie** side of life. You have a crisis or a difficult situation, you need to explain and talk about it and your aspie glazes over and asks you what time you'll be making dinner. You repeat how you feel, it's obvious your aspie didn't get the point of what you said. You state, without subtlety, that you are upset and need support.

Your aspie, devastatingly, says, 'Hmm, I know, you already said.' And they go back to what they were doing.

You challenge them and ask why they don't care, what about all the times you supported them? Doesn't it work both ways?

At this point, you may get some emotional reaction, as it is a good way of reminding the aspie that you're the one clearing up after their sensory blowouts and so, perhaps, you deserve some support in return. Or, you may get another terrible reply, like, 'Yes, but what can I do to help? There's nothing I can do is there?'

Logically, in so many situations, there *is* noting your aspie can do to help, so they lose interest and turn away. You've talked about your problem, they've ascertained there is nothing to be done and that's that.

Well, it is as bad as it sounds, frankly. Your aspie truly *is* turning away from you at this point. They *are* saying they can't or won't help and they're serious when they ask about dinner. There really is no limit to the selfishness sometimes.

From the **aspie** side of things, it is as logical as not being able to help you but there is more to it. Your stress and upset and wailing is so distracting from being an aspie. Sometimes, aspies are just getting through their day, being themselves and doing stuff that works and doesn't make the feelings muddy. Then you come and are saying all these things which make life complex and demanding and actually need a response from the aspie - a response that has nothing to do with the aspie themselves.

They don't want to deal with your drama. Life is full of drama, it's like always living on stage with the lights shining down and someone shouting, 'Cut!' just when you got to the good bit. You can never work out what's going on because no one gave you a script so it's a constant improvisation, with real-life consequences.

Then, on top of all that, the very person who is meant to make it all more bearable and shout cues from the front of the stage, *they* hop up onto the boards and start improvising too and expect you to join in! And they expect you to be able to be able to shout cues to them and make it all bearable.

When did that happen? When did it become the aspie's remit to sort out anyone else's problems? And anyway, how often have we offered you advice and had it laughed at or tossed away as impractical? Aspies don't forget, you know. It may be that the advice we gave before was laughable but we still offered it, we gave it thought and tried to help, in our way.

And now, after all that, with the drama of the stage and the previously unwanted advice, you now want us to step up and make it all better? Really?

Yes, behind very turning away there is a lot of anger, fused together with the stress of life itself and the belief that you should stay in your role as supportive other, the cue-giver who does not belong on the stage and should only be waiting to make life okay when the aspie cannot stand the glare of the lights for one more second.

Horrible, horrible aspie. If we were totally honest, we might offer up, 'I just don't care,' as our first response. In a way, it would be completely true. We don't have enough left to care about your problems because by caring, they become our own and we live them and see them and feel them. Most often, you see, it isn't a lack of empathy that plagues us but a mis-placed empathy that, once released, knows no bounds and will not go back in the box.

Better, then, to avoid helping in the first place and keep a tight grip on that Zen-like calm we hold so dear. Better to fob you off with an unkind word and hope you're feeling better soon, so that we don't have to worry we'll be alone on the stage.

Better that we don't give in to the panic and the rage and the suppressed emotions which sway us into the path of imminent disaster, suddenly, terrifyingly, taking you with us because it is *your* disaster this time and we have to come along for the ride.

Yes, behind every calm face and blank response is an aspie staring into the spotlights, wondering who lies behind in the unseen theatre. Where will the next voice come from? What shall we say this time? Will we have good lines or bad? What action takes us forward to the next stage of the story?

Forgive me, readers, I am an unkind aspie and perhaps your aspie is unkind too. Sometimes, the best you can hope for in the middle of a crisis is for your hand to be touched on the way past or for some flowers to be ripped from the garden and placed, in size order, in a vase where you might see them.

And sometimes, the last thing you want is an aspie trying to solve your problems because once we get a hold of something, we can't let go and you never know where you might end up. Better to stick with the flowers and just get on with making tea. It will be all right, so long as we are together.

WHEN WORLDS COLLIDE...HOW TO DEAL WITH NON-ASPIES

Tongue firmly in cheek here, people, but I thought it might be good to offer some simple guidelines on how aspies can deal with non-aspies, in different situations.

Firstly, **patience** is always in order. I know it can be hard to be patient with people who just don't understand what you're trying to tell them. Sometimes, it doesn't seem to matter how many times you go over and over the same idea, they don't know what you mean. It's almost as if they stop listening.

Obviously, if they listened properly in the first place, you wouldn't have to go on about it, but non-aspies never seem to learn this lesson. There you are, in full flood of something amazing, great, fabulous and, most likely, world-changing and what do you get? Half an ear, if you're lucky.

Yes, there have been other fabulous things you needed to share and it's worth admitting this to them, when they're being less than enthusiastic. But this time is different and you need their attention, just this once.

If you don't get their attention, try not to beat them into submission. I know it's hard, but leave it and come back to it later. That way, they relax and think you've given up or forgotten. This means you can wait until they're not expecting it and come at the subject from a different angle. Sneak up on it, like, and watch as they listen, only realising their mistake when it's too late to go back. It's worth waiting for.

In a work situation, if you find yourself with someone who is so far from the aspie viewpoint, it's like ponies and giraffes, then you may need to use different tactics. People who really, really don't understand you, often they don't want to either, so it doesn't matter how you say a thing, or how you try to be friends, they still won't respect you.

It can be confusing, as this kind of person is nearly always a lynch-pin of the organisation, someone you have to work with and who is important to your job and other people's. You must interact with them at the same time as observing the little sneer they keep just for you.

Please, fellow aspie, do not give in to temptation and smack the sneer off their face. For those gentler aspies, neither must you let the air out of their tyres or find out where they live and use interesting ways to make their lives more exciting. (Not yet, anyway).

No, you must beat this person in a much more important way: by making them not matter. You are never going to get rid of their sneer, it's there forever and will have been used on many people before you. The self-important person who makes your life miserable at work is a professional at this kind of thing. They can have you crying in the toilets before you know you're even going to do it. And they can torture you without batting an eyelid, still keeping on top of their job and their other relationships.

If you let them get to you, then you won't be keeping on top of your job or your relationships. You, dear aspie, will be off those rails and out the door. You know it's true. So, step back and let them give off their waves of sneery, negative energy, without letting it wheedle its' way inside your armour.

I know this is easier said than done and you won't always win. Sometimes, the presence of this type of person is enough to spoil a job and have you moving on. That could be for the best, but do try to work around them and ignore them first. As I said, they're never going to understand you and some of their behaviour is based on fear. They dislike anything different and are never going to be friends with you. Let them carry on in the ignorance of never having known what a good friend you could have been.

Family. Oh dear, family. Where to start? In my family, the non-aspies roam free, amongst the aspie, the leaning-towards-aspie, the eccentric-somewhere-on-the-spectrum and the-one-you-avoid-on-the-stairs. I'm sure a lot of aspie families are like this, if they're honest. The trouble is, they often aren't honest.

It surprises me how often people expect an aspie to have sprung, ready-formed, from the fresh green earth. This strange thing they have wrong with them is nothing to do with the Family. We never had anyone strange in the family before.

This is a lie, dear aspie. A big, horrible lie, cooked up to protect the current generations from having to remember and admit what they know about the previous ones, as well as shuffling aside any unpalatable facts about themselves.

When they look at you with anger, pity, despair or share a look with one another, console yourself with the thought that they, rather like the evil co-worker, don't know what they're missing. By refusing to acknowledge any common ground, they are denying themselves a chance for greater self-discovery and a more rewarding relationship with you, their kith and kin.

Now, in every family, no matter how unfriendly, there will always be an ally. Seek them out and befriend them. It's likely they've been waiting for an opportunity to support you. This is where odd aunts, or shunned cousins come in handy. They tend to be more up your street anyway and can help you feel supported in a less friendly family environment.

For those of you who already have supportive families, appreciate them. Hang on til I clear my throat. Cough, cough. APPRECIATE THEM!!!!

Yes, I am yelling at you. Do not moan that they don't understand you, do not wish they could make your life easier. Do not blame them when your day falls apart like old cabbage. They are the ones who will always be there for you and, just because they don't always get you, it doesn't mean they're not trying. Give them a chance. Love them. Explain things to them and let them explain things to you. Do not be a pain in the butt.

Yes, I know, as an aspie myself, it can be very easy to be a pain in the butt. We can do it just by wandering through to the kitchen in the morning and drinking that nice cup of tea someone made for us. Except they didn't, and they have to make it again.

There are so many little ways that we drive people to distraction, that when it comes to us being the ones who are irritated by others, we should step back and remember. We are usually the ones who get on other people's nerves, accidentally or simply by pushing on until they can stand no more. Do allow your supportive family and friends their moment of annoyance.

If they feel ticked off with you, don't take it as a personal slight designed to ruin your day. Do not remember it endlessly, ready to wheel it out the next time they annoy you. Put it in perspective for all the times you have probably annoyed them.

I see, looking through what I've written, that the word I started with covers most of the bases: Patience.

We need so much patience to deal with other, non-aspie, people, as they exist on a slightly different plane from the one we know so well. We meet in the middle somewhere, occasionally through a haze or mist. Others need patience with us and vice versa; it's the only way to go.

Of course, it doesn't always work out this way. In my case, it doesn't often happen as patience is one virtue I lost down the side of the sofa many years ago. I've tried looking for it but all I seem to come up with are pennies and old dog chocolates.

Still, it is what we should aim for, the patience to deal with others and help them to understand us. If we can keep meeting in the middle, a little patience goes a long way towards clearing the mist so we can reach out to one another.

When all else fails, just remember that non-aspies are never going to fully understand why the hippo is fluffy and blue, they are only going to see that hippos must be smooth and grey. Some things are difficult to explain, but if others can accept us as we are, then it's the least we can do for them.

OBSESSIVE BEHAVIOURS

Oh, obsession. Love it! Yes, I know it's probably on the top 3 hate lists for non-aspies, but find me an aspie who doesn't love a good obsession.

The buzz you get from it and the glorious feeling that you have found something so fulfilling and worthwhile, it's bound to carry you to new, great adventures and be a world-changing experience. Until the next obsession, of course.

This is the 'good' side of obsessive behaviours, even if it's only viewed as a good thing by the aspie themselves. There are other, less empowering behaviours which need to be included and from which many aspies suffer.

For the purposes of this book, OCD, obsessive compulsive disorders, are the ones I have talked about most. They come in many different guises but are essentially the same: the need to impose order on a crazy world.

Take the chapters here as a guide for every aspie has their own obsessions and obsessive behaviours. Don't feel that every odd thing your aspie does is linked to these though, as we can be odd without being obsessive. Sometimes, eccentricity is simply that and can be ignored, but do be on the lookout for any obsessive tendencies which have turned into something which seem to control the aspie and not the other way around.

And don't, whatever you do, mess with the order of the keys on the wall, or the boots in the hall, or the direction of the cutlery or that amazingly pongy heap of undergrowth which is coming alive on the dining room table. It's all very, very important you know.

OBSESSION, THAT GLORIOUS
THING WE ALL LOVE...

All aspies love it, apparently. It's the one word which seems to crop up again and again when you search the web for more info on Aspergers and behaviour. It usually carries along nicely with the 'little professor' comments, very often linked with boys, where the aspie is meant to rattle on about their pet subject, to the detriment of everyone and everything around them, often in an affected, grandiose, stilted, lordly or overly-intelligent manner. Have I covered all bases there?

Just to be clear, girl aspies are obsessive too. I often think my choice of dogs sums up my aspie-ness quite nicely. I have 2 border collies: collies are usually obsessive, hyper-intelligent, prone to anxiety, problem solvers, creative and have a tendency to wander off and do their own thing.

I think I prefer the definition of a collie personality to the definition of an aspie one, when you look at them side by side.

Yes, we get obsessed. I put up my little chubby hand and make no apologies for it. Why apologise? Obsessions are glorious, wondrous creatures which keep us company through the dark nights and walk by our side, day after day. When we are alone in a room full of people we know, our obsession is always there, sitting comfortably beside us, always allowed into our personal space, always there.

Our obsessions will never ridicule us, on purpose or by accident; they will never laugh behind their hand, or sigh, tut, roll their eyes or slump their shoulders as they go to clean up the latest thing we broke.

Obsessions don't just know us as our family and friends know us. They don't know us like our best beloved knows us. They know us like we know ourselves - better sometimes. Our obsessions see our souls, they watch the glimmer as we shine and dance through life. They know that within every stoney-faced look we give the world, there is the heart of a gentle warrior, beating their way through lands of fearsome dangers and uncommunicable hardship.

There is more, though. The other side of obsession, the side which has less to do with what we love and more to do with what we *know*.

Oh reader, I envy you. Are you one of those people who knows how often it's okay to look in the face of a stranger to see if they will smile back? Can you speak the language of the old woman who might only want the time but maybe wanted to talk? Can you tell the difference between someone asking if you are fine and actually wanting to know?

On a personal note, even in the most intimate of relationships, the aspie is unsure. Did our best beloved really mean they were okay with not going out? Why did they say *that* when they meant *this*? What happened between me coming downstairs and going up that made the atmosphere change?

Can you see it? All the questions? They form a little cloud of confusions and, like most clouds, if you have enough of them you get a bigger cloud and eventually rain. Or hail. Or snow.

The thing is, you see, obsessions do know us better than we know ourselves but, more importantly, we know *them*.

We know all about them. As you probably realise, to your sorrow, if you accidentally set us off or we find you when we're full of enthusiasm. We can tell you everything about them, endlessly, or in small pieces, like machine gun fire.

We can go on for as long as it takes.

And you want to know why? Why, for heaven's sake, why?! Why is that same cartoon, that same programme, the ants again, oh no, not the ants again! The pet subject, no matter the age of the aspie, can be the dread of the aspie-family and friends combo. But -

The reason why we are so happy to share our obsession is only partly because we are obsessed. The other part of that reason is a simple one: we understand the obsession. We are not confused. We can explain it to ourselves (very important) and then to you (another facet of explaining it to ourselves).

You know how 2 year olds ask the same questions over and over? The aspie obsession can be likened to that, but instead of us asking questions, we are explaining to ourselves, again and again. We are explaining what we know (we know something fully and completely, get the flags!) and we are confirming our knowledge.

And we are so excited about this full, unconfused and clear knowledge that we just had to share it with you. Again! And yes, we actually do know that we go on, but it's such good news, so exciting! So personal to us. Which means, dear reader, that *you* are personal to us.

When we share the obsession again, don't focus on the little things (that's our job), focus on the bigger picture. This sharing means the cloud of confusion has had its butt kicked out the door and we are clear and happy to share our important stuff with you, because we love you.

258

Translate it again, simplify, aspify - we tell you these things because **we love you**. Sometimes, it's the only way we can say those words.

So the next time you're being driven mad by us, look past the words to the gentle warrior inside. They battled untold horrors to get to this stage, to be able to look you (almost) in the eye and tell you what they love, because by telling you what they love, they're saying they love you.

And people, this is true of so many of our loved ones who haven't been hit by the aspie-ray, so do look past the prose to the poetry beneath.

IT'S A KICKER...LIFE AS AN ASPIE

I have a confession to make: I am a despicably unreliable person (in case you hadn't noticed). Obviously, I knew this already but I do tend to push it to one side and just get on with getting on, hoping for the best and trying not to dwell on my faults.

As you know, if you obsess over what you can't do and what you should have done but haven't, then the old self-esteem plummets and life becomes even harder. So, I've found it's best to ignore the very transitory nature of my reliability and move on.

The trouble is that life is full of surprises, unfortunately, and they have a tendency to kick you up the behind while you're looking at something else. Often, this swift, sharp kick carries with it some epiphany and we get a full-on, clear, no-holds-barred view of ourselves. And that's what happened to me today.

I needed to find an important email from years ago, but I wasn't sure when. Searching the emails by name came up with nothing (Hotmail just has a laugh at our expense so many times). So, I settled down to scroll through many, many pages of email history to find what I was looking for.

I needed to go back to 2007, which in email terms is like saying you're just popping out to see Cromwell and won't be a minute. I decided to look through my Sent folder, working on the logic that I would have sent far fewer emails than I received.

Yes, this was good logic except - and here comes the kick - the emails received are often from random people or groups, whereas emails sent are from yourself. By definition, this makes them all a lot more personal, even if a third of them are sharing funny quotes or Savage Chickens cartoons.

I'm an absolute sucker for nostalgia, it is a big thing with me and I have to avoid giving into it or I get nothing done and end up weeping quietly over old Christmas cards. Unfortunately, there is no avoiding some nostalgia when you have to scroll past all your old emails.

The first little kick was the cuddy-load of emails sent to my old school friend when she worked in an office. We got more gossipping done then than ever before. It never happens now as she left work to have her baby and didn't go back. We've lost touch and rarely talk more than twice a year.

The second kick was all the emails starting with 'Talk me down...' or 'You'll think I'm mad but...' or 'Can I run this past you?' and so on. Each one was some lovely new idea that was bound to succeed because it was just perfect and nothing could go wrong. Ahem.

My enthusiasm shone through even in the subject headings. I resisted the temptation to open a few and see if the ideas were still good as I knew I would only get caught up again and the freight train would be hurtling off down the hill before I knew what was happening.

I felt sad when I saw those subject headings. For instance, who on earth was ever, ever able to talk down an enthused aspie? Well, in my case, no one. The idea was too good, other people just couldn't see it, etc.

And as for me possibly being mad? Less said the better. And running an idea past someone is coming back to that freight train. It runs past people too and if they're standing too close they get sucked into the air flow and that's that. Also, it's very hard to have a proper look at an idea when it's moving at such a speed, so really I may as well have been talking to myself.

I glumly reflected that all my grand schemes have come to nothing and I still need to wait for money to come in before I can go shopping. Of course, if I had stuck with *one* of those ideas, to the exclusion of all else, who knows?

That's the trouble, though. What came through loud and clear was how often I went off into the sunset, waving my stick at the sky, happy I had cracked it at last. And then again. And again. In the end, I was relieved to realise I wasn't going to find the email and close down the program so I didn't have to look at myself anymore.

It's not all doom and gloom, though, as some of my plans did come off. Just some. As well as my tuition, I've done quite a few school workshops over the years, in creative writing. They featured strongly in the list as I sent out information and arranged visits. I was quite pleased to see those.

What was less brightening was the long list of jobs I applied for over the same time period. It does make you want to go back and tell yourself to **Stop It!**

In the middle of it all was a short email I had sent cancelling one school workshop. I gave illness as a reason, and it was, but not the whole reason. It was the time I lost my confidence and became terrified at the thought of going into another classroom. I came up against the brick wall and couldn't do it. I needed the money but I still couldn't do it. I didn't do any more workshops for about three years.

And the upside? Now I know *why* I came up against the brick wall. I was overwhelmed and didn't know it. I didn't possess the self-knowledge to understand I was being taken over by everything I was trying to do until I could barely get out of bed in the morning.

Between now and then I have come a very long way and am much more aware of my limitations. I am a little wiser and try to keep an eye on myself most of the time. It doesn't stop my grand ideas and running into sunsets, but it does tend to stop me before I reach the cliff. Or the wall.

I did go back into the classroom and realised, once there, that I had missed it and that I could still make a difference. I think this is the important lesson from today's scrolling through history - I have made a difference as I've gone along. For all my running about, my epiphanies, my need to be doing something else each time, I've changed things too and made some people feel a little better about themselves.

I don't mean that to sound big headed: I say it with an image in my mind of a little boy in one of my workshops who told me he couldn't write stories and didn't even like them. He said I should move on and not bother with him, then laughed cheerfully.

He wrote the most exciting story of a secret cave, full of magic treasures and adventure, with children who fought battles to survive with dragons and monsters. And with each small chunk written, he leapt up to come and show me then confide in me what would happen next.

It's thanks to people like him, with the light in his eyes as he rushed to sit down and write more, that I know all those emails were worthwhile. If I can't be reliable or methodical or any of the things which mean plenty of money for milk, at least I can open the window sometimes, to let in the summer breeze.

And we all make a difference, in our own way. As aspies, the normal, regular, usual things in life often get away from us and we can make life difficult for ourselves and other people. But this is because we are privileged to see behind the scenes, the unusual, the magical, the awkward and the mystical.

This is what we bring to our lives and the lives of others: a little bit of the extraordinary, wrapped up in cloth shoes that were never meant to be worn in the rain. No matter that we often have wet feet, so long as we bring some of the magic other people need. Even if they don't realise it.

THE DISTRACTION OF THE BUSY MIND: ACCESSING INFORMATION

Sometimes we all need to access information in our brains, vital snippets at the right time, or long periods of concentration for work or life events. Aspies can have real, sustained difficulty accessing information in a way that helps them release it into the world, so other people can look at it.

Some brains are accessed via books or the computer, the physical aid to being able to 'leave', while your body stays behind. For me, I need the extra distraction of a story, or computer game, to help my mind step sideways. I would be no good as a meditator, using silence and calm to connect with myself. I tried it and was surprisingly good at being able to bring my body to a meditative state: the mind was another matter.

I think that this need for a distraction, to almost trick your mind into doing something better, points to the aspergers trick of being at least two people at once. Everything is about layers: the outside world, the buffer we create between us and it, other people, people close to us, the persona we show them all, the persona we show ourselves, the real 'us' who ventures out when no one is looking, the 'us' we don't like, who takes over and ruins things, the 'us' we used to be, peeking round the corner of memory.

So many personalities and images, too many ways to interact with the world. Alongside this, we have the internal commentary of how to do things, when to do them, what to say, when to stop talking, when are they supposed to stop talking, is it okay to leave now?

Should I smile? Should I put my head down? Was I supposed to be listening? What do they mean?

These words, phrases, endless wondering, existing amongst our rack of personalities, waiting to be donned at the right occasion. Is it any wonder we often look confused?

So, it's no surprise that we need to be able to zone out or physically leave to be able to recollect ourselves, to access the brain in a different way, one which frees up what we know so we can use it to our advantage. And no surprise either, that we need a little nudge sometimes, to help us get there.

I've spoken before about the need to leave quickly and feel safe, to hide under the blanket, real or imaginary. That's the panic reaction to stress. What I mean now is a place we can retreat to at any time, to dip in and out and have that ounce of refreshment needed to help us get along and connect with ourselves, as a precursor to connecting with others.

Don't confuse the inability to access information with the amount of stress we're under, either. For instance, at home when I'm working or writing (you notice I don't count the writing as work), I often need to blend a few activities together to make it feel comfortable.

If I need to do work, admin or similar, I'll often combine it with other things on the computer, like checking the bank, Facebook, emails, playing games and so on. I know a lot of people multi-task on their computers, what I mean is, I find it very difficult to concentrate on the work without having all the other things going on at the same time.

When I'm writing, I do need to concentrate fully then, whether it's for this blog or my fiction. Once I start writing, that's it: it's the one activity I can do which is an end in itself and doesn't require a few other things running along with it to make it work. But I don't just sit down and start writing. I need to prepare for it, build up to it and often do all the same things beforehand that I mentioned above. It's as if I need my mind to rattle at full speed, doing all kinds of different jobs, before it can sit down and do only the one.

Out and about, when concentration is needed, I can be in trouble. After all, what is the on-the-hoof equivalent of playing games, checking emails, doing your bank and so on? If you actually need to be somewhere, speaking to someone and asking intelligent questions, what am I supposed to do to help myself concentrate then?

Well, I talk to myself, inside my head and keep an eye on me. It sounds mad, possibly, though I'm sure we all do it to some extent. It's an extension of those multiple personas I was talking about, but they try to work together at times when I need to be wholly present and accounted for.

An example would be, in a one to one conversation with someone official. How do I stop myself drifting off to look at the stain on the wall behind them, or fixate on the mole on their lip or suddenly remember I haven't turned my phone off and get lost rooting through my bag?

If I need to be *there*, I need the pep talk that goes with it. I'll have an internal monologue from the bossy, urgent voice, reminding me to concentrate, concentrate, concentrate. That's annoying but it does get my attention and make me re-listen - as by then I've stopped listening and that was why I was having to tell myself to concentrate.

Then there's the secretarial voice, listing what I need to remember to talk about. A physical list may also be in evidence, but the secretarial voice will be reminding me of how to broach things, what tone to use, how to get the best out of the situation.

Then the warmer one will always come in and remind me to try to make friends with the person, find common ground, treat them nicely, be attentive and not just concentrate, because people always prefer you to actually listen and not just fix them with your off-putting stare while you soak up their words.

Amongst all this I also have to behave like a semi-normal person and achieve whatever objective I set out to in the first place. I can come away from something like this filled with such a relief that I need to immediately go and buy chocolate, to celebrate.

You see, almost everything which requires proper thought has an unfortunate tendency to use your brains. And your brains are packed full of STUFF. What enormous amounts of information we need to keep on hand! It can be very hard to find what you are looking for when faced with boxes full of 'appropriate behaviours', 'correct phrases', 'acceptable expressions' and so on. Imagine having to squeeze past all that just to find the little box marked 'task for the day'.

The trick is, that by distracting those very brains with other things, like you can when you're at home, you instantly move the other boxes further apart and are able to dash across the brain room and right to what you needed.

Out and about, in our official conversation, the voices telling you what to do also help because, by having the running commentary, you are emphasising the information usually stored in the boxes. In other words, you have already *taken account* of the boxes, again leaving you free to dodge past them and reach what you want.

Without the inner words, reminding you of what you need to do and how to do it, you would have to clump through the darkened room, bouncing off the big box of 'too much staring', stubbing your toe on 'ill-timed giggles', trying to edge past 'sneeze on demand' without disturbing it.

You may be wondering by now, why not just clear my mind and do what needs to be done? Surely, it would be simpler to clean it all out and be free of it? No boxes, no inner monologuing, only what you need to be thinking about. Does that sound good?

Perhaps, though it sounds like it would echo. I can't function with a clear mind, it has to be full and busy. Other people may be the complete opposite, but I think it's true that a lot of aspies have the busy mind, even if they don't particularly want it. I do sometimes have a completely empty mind, but that usually means I've switched off.

In terms of distractibility, it's a blessing and a curse. Without it, I really wouldn't be the person I am and certainly wouldn't be able to function. Then there are times when life would be so much easier if I hadn't become distracted! I think, perhaps, one must almost count as good distraction, though the separation is probably imaginary.

It's finding what works for you. For me, it's tricking the mind into not realising it's about to impart information. I know I'm dithering about and doing things other than work, and often tell myself off. It's only with hindsight I realised I wouldn't have managed what I did without the 'free-time' before I started working.

Others need to find what works for them and use it when it's really needed. I have to say, all of the above is fine, in my life as it is right now. You can imagine how badly it would all fare in a full-time working life where, miraculously, other people concentrate *all day*. All day!!

I guess the lesson is, life itself has to fit *you*, just as your smaller, personal methods need to match what you need and want. Information stored and accessed is only valuable if you can bring it out and use it for your own good. If you can't get past the boxes, then you need to do some shifting around and clear a path through.

Often, we worry that the total de-clutter is needed, when it isn't. What we actually need is the right space and lighting to make it work for us. Then you don't need to worry about tripping and giving in to 'grimaces without reason'.

SO, ROUTINE IS AN ASPIE THING?

I'm not really arguing with this one. Routine can be a wonderful thing, a soothing counter-balance to the ways of the world. It can make you feel in control as well as reassure you that everything has a purpose and there won't be any nasty surprises.

But it's also a stick to beat us with. I've often heard other people go on about how their aspie won't deviate from a routine, how they couldn't do a certain thing because it clashed with the routine. I've even been accused of it myself, when I've not wanted to do something spontaneous because I could see the day stretched out ahead of me in a planned way.

I think the only time I've heard routine and aspies being seen as wholly positive is when some poor child is being shoe-horned into school and their parents say that the part their little aspie likes is the school routine, that they find it comforting. Any other time and the aspie who loves routines is seen as a fly in the ointment of this grand world, full of opportunity and diversity. Right?

Well...I'd like to put my hand up here and resist the temptation to poke you in the eye with it. You see, from my point of view, I say that the world in general also loves routine. That as much as you criticise the aspie for being a fixed creature, the world seems trapped in the same way.

For instance, what is routine exactly? To the aspie, it's the way that things should be done, either the way they are organised or thought of, or simply the events that make up any given day or hour. Routine is simply a word to hang lots of different things on which mean something to the person and which are often repeated.

For the world at large, routine means something being done over and over. The definition is:

A sequence of actions regularly followed; a fixed program.

So, to the world, the aspie follows a sequence of actions regularly, as if their lives exist within a fixed program. All right then, that may be true, but the whole world is the same!

This fixed program could apply to how we behave towards each other, from the small routines of how we greet one another to the more complex ones of how we should behave within conversations and social situations. Aspies do not follow the routines of social situations, both large and small - we are often in trouble because of this, so we know it's true.

The world is also routine when it comes to how we should progress through life. It is an accepted routine to go through school, get a job, progress in your career, meet someone and settle down and so on. These are seen as natural progressions in the world, the routine of life in so many ways.

The aspie may not be able to move through these stages in the same way or may stall and go back. In many ways, the aspie won't progress past the school part, as all of life is a learning experience and there is always something new to discover.

For the great journey of life, aspies buck the trend and don't usually follow the routine prescribed as the norm. Life goes on, people send their babies to nursery school and we all sing the same song, again.

The routine of dating is a big one, don't you think? Girls' magazines thrive on it, womens' magazines make a business out of the more seasoned daters who want to learn the rules for grown up dating and relationship ethics. To the aspie, this seems like an absolute miasma of confusion. Every rule seems written for a different handbook from the one we were given.

The smaller routines, like how to order in a restaurant, how you behave at the table, what you should and should not be doing with the knives and forks, how many napkins you're allowed to use and why no one else is washing the spoon with vinegar: all these little things, easily accessible to non-aspies, as a normal routine, have to be learned by the aspie.

If we don't follow the routine, we draw stares and are possibly accused of being too fixed in our silly routines to enjoy dining out - our routines involving having the right table, not sitting in the chair facing the other diners, having enough time to study the menu, calling to the waitress before she's ready to come back, asking for another glass, using all the napkins because you needed one for your lap, one to keep for after the meal, the one wet with vinegar so you could wash the spoon and the spare one just in case.

The routines of normal dining are broken up by the aspie routines of enjoyable/safe/healthy dining. The routines of conversation also fall foul of the aspie approach, as do so many other routines, encountered on a daily basis and treated as being what everyone does, until the aspie wanders along and ricochets through them, scattering them in all directions and wondering what the fuss is about.

You see, our silly routines, which are so important to us, are seen as a quirk of personality and they are an annoying quirk because we often follow them despite what is seen as acceptable. But I would ask, how is this so different from the routines imposed on us all by modern society? Why is it *not* a routine to do things in a certain way, but it *is* a routine for me to do things my own way?

What makes society the judge of a routine? Why does it see its own routines as normal behaviour, when so many aspies exist within society and probably don't do things the same way? Why are society's routines so rigid but must be followed when mine have to be pushed aside and dismissed?

Yes, I acknowledge that the routines within society are there for the benefit of a great many people whereas mine are just for me (and anyone else who wants a really clean spoon), but they are big and little brothers. Routine does not change to suit the moment: it either is a routine or it is not.

Don't pretend the big brother routine, grinning behind you in the playground is just what everybody does then call my little brother routine, hiding next to the fence, a silly obsession which helps nobody. They are part of the same family, you just have to take a better look at them.

The problem is that my routines are always going to seem very small compared to everyone else's and my arguments for keeping them are not as good as the arguments for following the ones other people like. This is why aspies keep to their routines in a more muted, private way, so as not to incur discussion or ridicule. If we know that you'll be embarrassed when we ask for more napkins, we'll be careful to ask when you're not looking, but we'll still ask.

Just remember, though, how uncomfortable you feel when we do something outside the norm and outside your comfort zone. It's not good, is it? That niggledy feeling at the back of your neck, like a cold finger just nipped you there. It's much better to feel happy and comfortable when things are done the right way, don't you agree?

Yes, so do we.

MISCELLANEOUS ASPIE-NESS

Frankly, my whole life is one long round of miscellaneous as-pie-ness, but this section is even more random.

I've included a few blog posts done more for fun than self-improvement, though there are always insights buried within.

Aspies in Space was inspired by the in-fighting amongst myself and my two sons, IT teen and RT teen. In so many situations, their fighting is split up by me, only for me to realise I have somehow made things worse. This is the way of life and it would certainly be the way of life if Aspies were in Space.

ASPIES IN SPACE

If aspies were in charge of a space ship, going on a super-important mission that meant life or death to everyone back on Earth, what do you think would happen? The fate of mankind hangs in the balance and the aspies have been chosen because, for whatever reason, they are immune to the catastrophe that has befallen the rest of the human race. Only we can save mankind, etc.

It would probably start well, with lots of good intentions and checklists. Aspies are often highly intelligent and the geekier ones would love the whole idea of living out the sci-fi dream. Yes, at last, we get to traverse the stars and meet robot overlords face to face. Finally!

Then the arguments would start about whose turn it was to press the trash-chute button. I can guarantee that something like this would be the first sign of instability. It would be nothing major. A small thing, the smell of uncompacted bananas mouldering behind the corridor wall would be enough to set it off.

Aspie Glen in sector 2 would deny it was his turn to press the button but Aspie Boot from sector 9 would have the job list to prove it was Glen's turn. Aspie Derek from sector 5, who had always wanted to look after the trash button, would wade in and make things worse by letting his latent jealousy get the better of him.

Aspie Susan from sector 1 would find a small tussle had broken out next to the trash button, with Glen repeatedly pressing the button to prove he was fine with doing it while Derek fought to reach the button and Boot did all he could to stop him reaching it, because it wasn't his job and it wasn't on the list.

Being the calming influence she is, Susan will immediately tell Glen he has now broken the button and they will all have to manually compact the trash, which involves a small bucket and a hand held macerator. Glen will start crying and go to his room.

Boot will have decided by now that the whole thing was Derek's fault and they won't speak for the next four years, until the time Boot finally discovers that Derek has the last surviving copy of Dungeon Keeper, as well as the appropriate cosplay gear.

Susan, content she has scared the living daylights out of them, will re-set the trash button and get rid of the smell of rotten banana. She will then forget to go back and finish what she was doing and the whole mission will fail because of it, leaving the Earth to whatever fate awaited it and meaning that the human race now consists of a space ship full of aspies, most of whom don't actually like each other and at least half of whom would prefer to mate with robot overlords anyway.

Yes, when it comes to saving the world and/or the universe, aspies will have the right idea but, for the most part, the wrong personality-type to get it done. For all that so many of us love things like Star Trek, you never found Captain Kirk obsessing over his RPG holographic unit - he only ever wanted the real-life experiences and very often got them.

Mr Spock, perhaps the one people may think of as a latent aspie with his coolness of demeanour and difficulty with emotions, was actually a highly efficient officer, always able to save the day and a counter-point to Kirk's unashamed lechery. Spock was just cool, people, he wasn't an aspie. He had control of his emotions, he wasn't repressed.

If Mr Scott had been the aspie, there would never have been anyone to refuse to push the engines a little harder or to hand out the malt whisky. He would have given in and pushed the engines too hard, the ship would have exploded or broken and he would be permanently drunk, as a reaction to the stresses of life.

The true aspie in the equation was always Dr McCoy. He hated the transporters, even though he knew how they worked and why they wouldn't vaporise him. He was argumentative and fond of telling people what he would and wouldn't do. He was always speaking inappropriately to Spock, pointing out his physical and emotional attributes. And given any encouragement at all, he fell in love (without the lechery) and then, usually, the lady in question would die or turn into a monster.

So, you see, to be successful the space ship has to have non-aspies in abundance, with only one aspie to spice things up. Isn't that right? Isn't life like that?

To function, do we need more non-aspies than aspies? Do we need aspies to be in safe places, away from buttons that operate more than the trash? (Does anyone else know they would push a big red button, no matter what it did, if they had to stand near it for long enough?)

I would like to say that aspies could save the world on the illustrious space ship. I would love to promise you that we wouldn't be petty enough to make the mission fail because we fell out over little disagreements. I would also like to attest that a mass gathering of aspies, forced to live together, would not fall into anarchy. Actually, no, I can definitely attest to that one as anarchy requires a sustained level of action and rising up against something. Come on, we're not going to manage *that*.

I think, given the right support, we'd be pretty happy on the space ship, though. So long as we didn't hold the fate of the world in our hands and didn't always have fights over the trash buttons. Imagine, floating through the stars, surrounded by technology and only the quiet peace of computers doing all the organised, methodical, attention-to-detail stuff on our behalf.

Perhaps, if the human race was reduced to a ship full of aspies, we could make a decent go of it. There would be hiccups along the way, but with the right checks and balances and no enormous red buttons linked to self-destruct mechanisms, we would probably be okay.

Also, we would always, always be ready to believe the impossible and so would never be surprised by what space threw at us. Sentient goo? Naturally. Brains as big as planets? Why not? A peaceable race of aliens that wants to be our friends and invites us onto their planet?

Are you kidding? We'd never fall for that one!

ASPIE APOCALYPSE AND HOW
IT'S NEVER OUR FAULT

The aspie stands alone, face turned to the setting sun as the walls tumble around him and the lights click out, one by one, along the darkened streets. The world as he knows it has ended and he is left, deserted, in a place no one can call home. He looks around, finally realising what has happened and wonders, How did it come to this?

I'll tell you: it started with a click.

The aspie has had enough of the clicking sound the washing machine makes, so comes to see what can be done about it. The noise only happens when the drum turns. In desperation, after trying a few cycles, he realises the machine is faulty.

Some time later and the machine is empty, with a spanner wedged between the frame and the drum so the aspie can fit his hand down the gap (don't try this at home, children).

The best beloved comes home to find the kitchen floor flooded from the piles of sopping wet washing and the aspie trapped in the machine, with his hand changing colour. He refuses help until he has found the source of the click.

The click turns out to be caused by the toggles on the tracksuit bottoms he likes to wear. As he will *only* wear tracksuit bottoms, there is always at least one pair in the wash, so it always clicks as the drum goes round. Having been enlightened by a furious best beloved, it is discovered that the hand cannot be released without the aid of the Fire Brigade.

One of best beloved's fantasies comes to life as a bundle of big, burly firemen surge through the door and into the kitchen. Unfortunately, the rest of the fantasy is unfulfilled because there's an angry aspie in the middle of the firemen, denying all responsibility for this predicament because how was he to know the annoying noise was from the washing?

Some small time later and the aspie is free, with advice to call at the hospital and have the pale purple hand checked out by professionals. Big, burly firemen leave, almost followed by best beloved who has had enough and only wanted to come home to a cup of tea and a little bit of the favourite soap on TV.

Instead, they now have to pull the shoes back onto those tired feet that have spent all day working so that the aspie can have a life they can cope with, rather than being out in the world, going mad and attacking little old ladies in shopping queues.

On the way to the car, the best beloved points this out to the aspie, who is still moaning about his hand and the toggles on his trousers. Aspie flounces back to the house, refusing to get in the car with best beloved who should have more patience when a person is in need of medical attention.

Best beloved makes comment that the person will be *more* in need of medical attention if they don't flipping well shut up about something they brought on themselves and should have had the brains to avoid in the first place.

More arguments ensue, followed by the aspie gesticulating wildly and hurting hand even more on the bannister rail as they try to make a grand exit up the stairs. Screaming follows as aspie believes hand has fallen off, pain is so bad. Best beloved considers pulling the hand off altogether and putting an end to the whole performance, but instead persuades the aspie to sit down and shut up.

Aspie does sit down and shut up and, thereafter, refuses to speak, choosing instead to have a high sulking session over the sore hand, lack of sympathy, the fact that their own trousers are to blame, the other fact that they didn't get to see the fire engine arrive with the lights flashing and the sorrowful state of affairs with best beloved going on about the bad day, as if it is *their* day that has gone wrong and not the aspie's.

Later, best beloved is faced again with the dreadful kitchen, puddles everywhere, all the clothes needing washing again and nothing to wash them in because the firemen had to break the machine to release the aspie's hand.

Silence ensues from best beloved who decides a night away would be the best thing and maybe, you never know, when they return in the morning, the kitchen could be cleaned up by a reluctant, but willing, aspie.

Words are said to this effect, to the monolith on the stairs, who only hears that the best beloved is leaving them and, to add insult to their injury, also wants them to do all the housework in the entire house before tomorrow morning.

Aspie monolith rouses self to speak, to point out that he cannot possibly do all that work, especially with a bad hand and it's probably better if the best beloved stays away, as they obviously don't want to be here.

This, on top of the hand, the firemen, the wet kitchen and the aching feet is too much. Best beloved packs their bags and leaves, hoping the mother won't go on too much about them being back in their old bedroom again.

Aspie, alone on the stairs, with no one to help look after their bad hand, may not actually be standing in the middle of a ruined civilisation, but it will feel like that to them. Those feelings, so rarely seen on the outside, will be roiling like drowning horses within them, to the point that whole worlds collapse within the heart of the deserted aspie.

They will be the sad, doomed hero of their own story, with not an ounce of blame on their shoulders. Well, perhaps they will concede *some* blame for the broken washing machine, but everything else was caused by the best beloved taking it all completely personally and not making any allowances for the aspie needing special treatment.

Once this period of dramatic sulking is at an end, the aspie will realise their hand really does need medical attention as it seems to have changed colour again. At about 3.30am, faced with riding in an ambulance or bringing down the wrath of their best beloved, they call b.b's mother's house and beg for help.

So, hours after the event, the best beloved forgives, yet again and comes out of bed to collect a contrite, but not vocally apologetic aspie and take them to hospital. The hand is saved (it was only a sprain) and so is the relationship. Complete doom is averted, thanks to the best beloved's ability to come round in the face of all-out provocation and also thanks to the aspie, in the end, for knowing which side their bread is buttered.

Reader, the aspie is not always a misunderstood, wounded animal. They can be the most aggravating creature and can combine real and actual need with absolute selfishness. When things go wrong and they are afraid or upset, the whole world pivots on its axis and begins to revolve around them. They will not, or cannot, see the other point of view at this stage. It is all about them.

When things calm down and they have been left to their own devices, some normality returns and things can be salvaged from the wreckage of either total meltdown, or massive sulk - or both. This salvage operation really does depend on the non-aspie being willing to recover from whatever has gone on in the dramatic stage of the action and to forgive the aspie enough to not want to lock them in a cupboard and poke them with a sharp stick through a special hole in the door.

I can only say, thank you non-aspies, and bless you best beloveds. Gosh, but we can be pustulous, ungrateful creatures, ready to get ourselves into trouble without a second thought, then willing to blame others for us being there, even when they're trying to pull us back out.

I would like to offer some rational, kind reason why we behave like this. I can say that all the usuals apply, like stress, confusion and dangerous curiosity, but really, when things like this happen I think it's a sign that the aspie needs to remember they are responsible for their own destiny and that best beloveds do not grow on trees.

It also serves as a reminder to best beloveds not to take everything the aspie throws at them. Sometimes you need to throw it back, or at least soak it in onion juice and hide it under their pillow to teach them a lesson.

Relationships are based on give and take, but it has to be from both sides. When the drama happens, as it inevitably will, count to ten, leave the house, eat chocolate, visit your mother and come back without doing anything rash in the meantime.

And aspies, dear aspies, please do sometimes consider the consequences of the proverbial hand in the washing machine drum. There won't always be a team of big, burly firemen to help you out of it. And next time, your best beloved may not come back from their mother's.

A GUIDE TO YOUR ASPIE

So, you have your new aspie and are wondering what to do with him/her. Depending on size and gender, some of these instructions may need to be followed with caution but we are confident that you will be able to get the best out of your aspie for many trouble-free years to come!

(Disclaimer: we are not responsible for any physical, emotional or financial harm that may come to you when following these instructions. Once unboxed, your aspie is not eligible for our guaranteed swappage and refurbishment policy. Please have a good look at the aspie through the window provided before unboxing).

1. Unbox carefully and without making physical contact with the aspie. Pull down the box using the flaps provided and allow them to step free by themselves.

2. Allow your aspie free rein, to explore their surroundings. For ease of capture, we recommend not unboxing in an area that is too large or too small. Open fields would not be suitable, unless you are a long distance runner. Small rooms are to be used at your own risk.

3. Do not ask the aspie what they want, until they initiate conversation as this is likely to set off the finely-calibrated temper-tincture.

4. When your aspie has stepped free of the box and begun to show some curiosity about their surroundings, then you may ask them if they would like a drink or something to eat. Offer one thing at a time, closely followed by the choice of drink or food.

5. Do not be surprised if the aspie follows you closely and makes it awkward to prepare the food and drink. Aspies are wary of physical contact but, quixotically, are very good at getting under your feet and being trodden on.

6. If you tread on the aspie, immediately accept responsibility. In no way blame your aspie, even if it was their fault, or you will hear about it for years to come.

7. Be prepared for them to choke/force down/suffer their food and drink as you 'did it wrong'. Note: You will need to have your

aspie for many years before you are able to do their food and drink the right way, so do not worry too much about this.

8. Do not expect to introduce your aspie to your family and friends anytime soon. If you have already arranged a surprise get-together, to welcome them, then you are either very brave or have the hind of a Rhino. Good luck.

9. When your mother calls around 'as she was passing' to meet your aspie, do not be surprised if your aspie changes personality. As usual, extremes are in evidence and there will either be a switch to complete charm or the charm of a mosquito.

10. Be prepared for this first encounter to colour your aspie's relationship with your mother and everyone else you know for the foreseeable future. If your aspie was charming, then everything that happens afterwards will be your fault. If your aspie was a mosquito, then they'll never be able to do any right and that will also be your fault.

11. If you have romantic designs on your aspie, I suggest you develop an extra patience gene or take up the drink. You'll be need-ing both at some time, probably together. (Please note: we cannot offer detailed instructions on the best way to romance your aspie as everything we tried either worked or failed for no apparent reason. Again, good luck).

12. Sleeping arrangements: Your aspie must not be too warm, or too cold, too tired before they go to bed or too wide awake. You must not wake them just after they settled down, even if they weren't asleep to begin with. You must be able to tiptoe like Tinkerbell and

be able to control and resolve every noise issue within a 50 mile radius. You must also keep an eye on the weather (wind blowing and rain tapping are the most difficult) and you must not snore or talk in your sleep as, like The Princess and the Pea, your aspie will be able to detect any noise *you* make from any part of the house, even if you sleep in a tent in the garden.

13. Computer arrangements: Your computer no longer belongs to you and you should ensure, preferably before your aspie is delivered, that you have the highest spec package in computer equipment and internet access that money can buy. Also, if you buy a laptop as well as a computer, expect the aspie to need that too, because the keyboard is better for long typing and you wouldn't want to be selfish and hog it to yourself, would you?

14. Pets. In general, aspies can be great animal lovers so have some hope your aspie can live in happiness alongside your furry friends. This advice does not always apply to big, jumpy dogs or biting cats, so if your pet is likely to initiate unwanted physical suffering on the aspie, do try to train the animal as well as yourself, on how to behave. (Note: biting cats will not be trainable, they will merely take greater pleasure in biting the aspie for fun. The cat will probably need to go live with your mother.)

15. Housework. You are on your own with this one. In theory and under controlled conditions, aspies are more than capable of doing housework and maintaining some order. In practice, this would mean leaving them a list; you remembering the list and explaining it to them; or being able to push forward with the list de-

spite it being a prearranged chat-time with online friends, an anniversary of an obscure 80s game, the time of the day when they don't feel like it, the list that *you* made and they didn't so what happened to their list? and the very minute they were inspired to do many, many creative things which you now want to ruin with your typical selfishness.

16. Temper-tincture. As mentioned earlier, this is finely calibrated and you should avoid sudden movements or unnecessary disturbances. The tincture may need to be shaken up and run around the room with before the aspie is able to calm down. Occasionally, loud wailing, screaming, wall-biting and pandemonium must accompany the running around. Take cover until it is calm, accept full responsibility and put the kettle on.

17. Communication: Again, we have found many contradictions with this one and we think the aspie communication centre must be self-governing. We have tried to fix it many times and it reverts to a set pattern of stubborn awkwardness and the inability to process dull, practical information. We apologise for this and hope you will be patient with us. If you have any particular difficulties with communication, we recommend following the last instruction of number 16 (this is applicable to many situations, do not be afraid of overuse).

18. Making your aspie happy: Despite all the inherent difficulties outlined in our guidance, we firmly believe it is possible to make your aspie very happy indeed. The key is in following this list as accurately as possible while keeping up good communication

with your aspie. You have not made an easy decision, in bringing your aspie home, but with some effort and imagination, you can have a rewarding relationship for many years to come.

For much more aspie-ness, advice and regular updates from the world of Aspergers, please visit http://aspie-girl.blogspot.co.uk search Amanda J Harrington on Amazon or visit www.thewishatree.com